FAITH
– AND –
YOU

Other books by Terry Pluto

False Start

Everyday Faith

*Champions for Life: The Power of a
Father's Blessing* with Bill Glass

The View from Pluto

Unguarded with Lenny Wilkens

Our Tribe

Crime: Our Second Vietnam with Bill Glass

Browns Town 1964

Burying the Curse

The Curse of Rocky Colavito

Falling from Grace

Tall Tales

Loose Balls

Bull Session with Johnny Kerr

Tark with Jerry Tarkanian

*Forty-Eight Minutes, a Night in the Life
of the NBA* with Bob Ryan

Sixty-One with Tony Kubek

You Could Argue But You'd Be Wrong
with Pete Franklin

Weaver on Strategy with Earl Weaver

The Earl of Baltimore

Super Joe with Joe Charboneau and Burt Graeff

The Greatest Summer

FAITH
– AND –
YOU

Terry Pluto

Gray & Company, Publishers
Cleveland

I believe in the Biblical concept of tithing: ten percent of
everything I earn from this book will be donated to Akron's
Haven of Rest City Mission.

Gray & Company, Publishers
1588 E. 40th St.
Cleveland, OH 44103-2302
www.grayco.com

ISBN 1-59851-015-0
Printed in the United States of America
First printing

To Harry Watson, chaplain at Summit County Jail . . .
I want to be like you when I grow up.

Contents

Introduction

What does this have to do with me? We've all asked that question while sitting through a sermon or reading a spiritual book.

What's the point? Why does it matter? How can this help me or anyone else connect with God or improve our lives?

Those aren't selfish questions. They go to the heart of what most people want—an Everyday Faith that can help us act and possibly get an idea what God wants from us.

I really believe that's why so many people have responded so positively to my "Everyday Faith" column in the *Akron Beacon Journal,* and to the book of those columns published under the same title in the spring of 2004.

People who haven't been to church in years, people who have given up on church, and people who are very committed to church often tell me, "Keep writing about this; you are talking about my life."

That's what real faith writing should do—address real life.

That's what I hope these twenty-eight essays will do. I first wrote about some of these themes in the *Beacon Journal* and have expanded those pieces here. Others are completely fresh. My goal is to have something in all of them that can help people who want a stronger connection to God. Perhaps there will be something here for people who aren't afraid to admit they sometimes feel distant from God, or for those who wonder why they are in the middle of some mess that just won't go away. I write for people like me—people who sometimes struggle and become frustrated with themselves, people who occasionally have experienced the warmth of God's smile and that inward sense of peace from knowing that they're doing what God would have them do.

I write for people who may have been hurt by someone in church, people who have been discouraged by one who claimed to speak for God (and maybe did so in a voice that shook the walls and broke the heart). I write for people who have found contentment in their faith, but want a deeper relationship with God.

I don't have all the answers to faith questions. I don't quote a Bible verse or an old saying without context. I won't enter into a vague spiritual discussion or wander into the middle of a theological spitball fight between religions and denominations.

I don't write about abortion, gay marriage, or the other religious hot-button issues. You can find thousands of opinions about those topics, and I sincerely doubt that anything I write will change anyone's mind. I have nothing new to add to the debates.

In this book I write about lending money to friends or relatives. Is that a good idea? And I write about counting your blessings. You can do it, and I tell you how.

Do you want to try to find a church? I have some suggestions. Does how and how much you tip people say anything about your faith? I think so.

Why do we find it so easy to believe damaging gossip? Why can't I just be quiet and listen to someone who simply wants to talk? Why do I find it so hard to take a day off? A real Sabbath is more than just going to the church or temple. These are some of my topics.

This book is about finding faith to face the day and trying to live that day the right way. I write as much about my failures as my triumphs, because that is what a life of faith is about. It's often as much suffering as celebration, with lots of mundane, uneventful stuff in between.

I'm a sportswriter, not a theologian. I never imagined being a faith writer. I'm still amazed when I speak in churches, or when people come to me with questions about faith. I've been writing about faith issues now for nearly four years. As I continued to write my faith columns for the paper, I sometimes have been frustrated because I had more to say about a topic, but space in the newspaper is limited. That's why I was eager to write this book.

Faith and God are big subjects, and I'm just a little voice. I do know that every voice does count and is heard by God, which is why I can write this book and feel eternally grateful to anyone who reads it.

FAITH
IN GOD

God Believes in Us

I sometimes go through life with the feeling that I'm not quite measuring up. I could do better. I should have seen that coming. I never should have said that. I should be smarter, tougher, gentler, less opinionated.

I can be my own worst critic, and I do it at the absolute worst times.

I need to remember that God believes in me even more than I believe in me.

Some of us grew up in religious settings where God was portrayed like the IRS agent from Hell. Your life is an income tax return, he has the green eye-shades and the calculator, and he's searching for one comma out of place, one mistake in addition, one iffy deduction that will cause a massive audit leading to your financial destruction. Or if you are an athlete, God can seem like a coach critiquing game films of your life. Any athlete will tell you that some of those film sessions crack their confidence. The good is rarely praised, just expected.

The bad is played over and over, the theme being, "How dumb can you be?"

You see the play once, twice, three times.

It's always the same. You always mess up. The coach may correct you from one angle, then another and another. Nit-picking is the order of the day. The result is a sense of being used as a human punching bag. In the dark of those film rooms, even 350-pounders who can pick up a tank begin to shiver and stutter as the coach calls out their names and asks how they missed that block, failed to make that tackle, or didn't notice they had started the play in the wrong place.

I'm writing this at the end of a week when I feel as if I've lost my edge as a writer. My stories were done on time, and they were done professionally. But they had about as much snap as a soggy bag of potato chips. I read my own stories and get bored fast, which makes me wonder why anyone would want to read them. Maybe after twenty-seven years as a sportswriter I'm just washed out. And as for writing about faith, who am I kidding?

I really believe that down deep, most of us fear that we will be uncovered as a bit of a fraud; that we aren't really what most people believe us to be. We're not a great parent, not an especially good spouse. When it comes to the job we're feeling like we're just hanging on.

That's why we need to hear that God believes in us more than we often believe in ourselves. I have to keep telling myself that. I have to believe it when I can't feel it; believe it even when it seems no one believes in me.

So now it's confession time: I have no theology degree. I've never studied under any famous religious leaders. I make no claim to understand everything about the Bible or even most things about life. For a long time I saw God as "The Grand Designer in the Sky," the one who started the universe in motion and now just sits back and observes what happens like we would watch a football game or a favorite TV show.

I make no claim to know everything—or even most things—about God.

But I remember that my wife had a major auto accident in 1995. She was driving on a two-lane blacktop road in rural North Carolina, returning home from visiting her parents. It was early morning. A car pulled in front of a gravel truck traveling fifty-five miles per hour in the opposite direction. The truck driver slammed on the brakes, jackknifing the truck right in front of my wife's Honda Civic. She never had a chance. That's exactly what the first police officer at the accident told me.

"When I saw what was left of the car and I saw the size of the truck, I was sure it was a fatality," he said. "I still don't know how she got out of that."

The driver of the truck pulled her out. Roberta suffered two broken ankles, one of which needed surgery. But the accident could have—and should have —been so much worse. But God was there for her. For us.

When most of us seriously think about our lives we have stories like mine. Maybe not quite as dramatic, but there is a situation that seemed so severe we were sure we'd never get out of it.

Somehow, we did. We're still not sure exactly how it happened. Some money showed up; a debt was forgiven; a job or promotion or raise came through. Something happened at the last possible moment. God was there.

In some church circles, they say, "God is always on time— but rarely early." They'll tell you that's because God wants us to know he came through.

Dr. Diana Swoope from Akron's Arlington Church of God once said in a sermon: "Our God is such an on-time God; He can show up late and make it seem early."

When that happens, God is whispering, "I believe in you more than you believe in you."

Talk to any alcoholic or anyone who suddenly is in a dangerous position chasing an addiction. Many of these people are not sure exactly how they beat their problems. Or how they escaped frying their brains, destroying their bodies, making themselves unemployable, their lives unlivable. Somehow, they go on. And in some cases, life is getting better, one day at a time.

That's how it is for me. I grab my faith, as small and shaky as it may be, and I take one step, then another, then another. I realize that God believes in me.

One of my favorite stories is in the New Testament book of Mark, 9:14–32. A man has a son who "is possessed by a spirit that robs him of his speech . . . it throws him to the ground. He foams at the mouth, gnashes his teeth and becomes rigid."

The man brings the child to Jesus, explaining that he had first taken the boy to Jesus' disciples, but they failed to help.

Jesus seems to moan as he says, "O unbelieving generation, how long shall I put up with you?"

Most of us have had times when we felt God heard our prayers and said exactly that: "How long shall I put up with you?" We expect to have the spiritual door slammed in our faces as if we were salesmen who had knocked in the middle of dinner.

But Jesus has something else to say: "Bring the boy to me."

The boy is in the middle of another of his scary, destructive attacks—growling, foaming, and rolling on the ground.

"How long has he been like this?" asks Jesus.

"From childhood," says the man. "It has often thrown him into fire or water to kill him. But if you can do anything, take pity on us."

Jesus replies, "Everything is possible to those who believe."

Mark's account says the boy's father immediately blurts out, "I do believe, but help me overcome my unbelief."

That is one of the most honest prayers in the Bible or anywhere else. God loves a prayer like that. It's not long and flowery. It's not full of pride and pretension. It's nothing but a plea from a desperate, discouraged, hurting father who really isn't sure if anything will happen to change his life or cure his son. He has seen Jesus heal others; that's why he brings his son to him.

The man has talked to the disciples (sort of like some modern-day clergy), and nothing has changed. But he doesn't quit. And when he faces Jesus, he knows he is in a godly presence. But the man has been rejected and disappointed so many times by so many people in his quest to help his son, he doesn't know what to believe.

The man in the Bible is like many of us. It seems the only time anything changes, it gets worse. Everyone we know is tired of hearing our problems. Sometimes we're so tired we can't even talk about our problems anymore. We become convinced we either brought them on ourselves or did something to deserve them. We feel cursed.

We need to know that God understands that feeling. Much of the Bible is the story of God reaching out to the people he loves while they withdraw in fear, back away in misunderstanding, or simply have no interest in anything but themselves. Which is how many people react to us when we're in a crisis.

I often pray like the man did in Mark's Bible passage: "I do believe, but help me overcome my unbelief."

I've told God that I'm hanging by a spiritual and emotional thread. I've told God that I'm not sure about all of what I believe anymore, but I have enough faith left to come to him one more time. I've learned to go to God when I've been in such anguish I couldn't sleep or I could barely speak. I have to remind myself that before I ask God for anything else, I must ask him for more faith . . . Everyday Faith to cope.

That was what touched Jesus about the man's prayer. It was a plea for more faith.

Mark writes that Jesus healed the boy, and then left with his disciples. The disciples asked him why they couldn't cure the boy of whatever was plaguing him. Jesus says, "This kind [of demon] can come out only from prayer."

Often, I don't pray enough or with enough confidence. I'm not sure God really wants to hear me. I remember someone telling me many years ago, "Don't you know God is busy with the universe? He'll get to you when there's time."

That sounds like a theology based on taking a number and praying that God is in a good mood when your turn comes.

Instead, I love the advice that Moses gives to Joshua in Deuteronomy 31:1–8. Moses is blessing Joshua to lead the Jews in their final journey into the Promised Land. Moses says, "The Lord himself goes before you and will be with you. He will never leave you or forsake you. Do not be afraid, do not be discouraged."

God speaking through Moses says those words because he knows there will be times when Joshua will be afraid, when he will be discouraged, when he will feel alone.

We all have those days. That's when we really need our Everyday Faith, when we need to remember that God is there for us and that God believes in us.

2

It's Okay to Enjoy Life

Do you get tired of people who say they have faith but act like they go through life with inflamed hemorrhoids? They sigh a lot. They grimace. They shake their heads sadly at the state of the world. If they ever did smile, you'd swear their faces would crack. If someone laughs, that means they must be doing something wrong. Pass the spiritual prune juice, because these people have a constipated view of life that is contagious.

There are too many people who think having faith means they can't have a good time. Their faith comes down to what they *can't* do, instead of appreciating what God has given us to enjoy. I thought of this when I heard a sermon by Dallas pastor Tony Evans who said, "There are a lot of trees in the garden."

So what?

Evans talked about the garden of Eden, the fall of Adam and Eve, and the way they were tempted by Satan. It's the first story about the first people in the first book of the Bible. Adam and Eve live in the garden of Eden. They can talk to God at any time. It's the closest thing there has ever been to heaven on earth.

Most of us know what happened. God told Adam and Eve not to eat of one tree in the Garden, the Tree of Good and Evil. The devil comes along in the form of a snake, starts to hustle Eve with a variety of temptations: Did God *really* say not to eat from that tree? Don't you know why? Because God doesn't want you to enjoy it.

It's kind of what some people tell kids: Do you know why your parents don't want you to get drunk? To get high? To have sex? Because they want to keep it for themselves! They know it will make you feel good. They know if you start doing such things you won't want to listen to them anymore. It's not about your parents looking out for you; it's about them keeping you down so they can stay on their power trip.

Since the beginning of time, the basic sales pitch for disaster hasn't changed, just the details.

While most of Evans's message was about the strategies of the devil, he said something I had never considered before despite having read the Adam and Eve story at least twenty-five times.

"There had to be more than one tree in that garden," Evans said.

He talked about there being lots of trees, very good trees, and how the devil convinced Adam and Eve to focus on the one thing they weren't allowed to have.

That happens to all of us.

Then it hit me. It's okay to enjoy ourselves. God gives us lots of trees.

Immediately, some people will think that means we should stick with the "church and temple tree." Or maybe the "good works tree." Want to stay out of trouble? Stay in church, serve the poor, and don't ever eat anything that tastes good. Suffer, that's what you need to do! That's why some people turn our relationship with God into drudgery. They make God into a slave master who will never be pleased with us. The best we can do is hope he'll tolerate us.

But God wants us to enjoy a life of faith. Yes, the world can be an ugly, demanding, frustrating place. Yes, people can do some very stupid and selfish things. Yes, life is sometimes not very fair. But there also are times when life is good, when the blessings flow.

Ever hear someone say, "This pie is so good, it's sinful?"

Well, it is only if we eat the *entire* pie. Otherwise, it's a gift from God for us to savor.

In John 15:11, Jesus tells his followers: "These things I have spoken to you so that joy may remain in you, and that your joy may be full."

He also said in John 10:10: "The evil one comes to steal and destroy, I have come so that you may have life, and have it to the full."

Jesus went to parties. He liked to eat meals and hang out with his friends. He didn't spend every waking moment healing the sick and soothing the broken-hearted. As my wife sometimes reminds me, "Even Jesus went to the mountains to pray and relax."

He probably checked out all the God-given trees, so don't be afraid to eat the fruit of some of the trees that God made for us.

How about the Dairy Queen tree? The golf tree? The hiking tree? The motorcycle tree? The talking on the phone with a best friend tree? The sitting around and watching cartoons with the kids tree?

Or—dare we say it—the nap tree?

The watching a game on the TV tree is good, as long as we don't think we have to watch *every* game. There are book trees that can be very comforting. We don't have to spend every waking moment memorizing Bible verses or slogging through the deep, confusing parts of scripture. We can just do nothing for a little while. We can read a John Grisham novel. We can grab a cookbook and make something just for fun.

Anything done to excess can become sinful. Men who watch ESPN day and night and avoid connecting with their families or doing their jobs have a problem. Women who are stuck on soap operas have a problem. Then there's gossip. Gossip is a killer of many of the trees that God has planted for us. Men and women fall prey to gossip.

Isaiah is an Old Testament prophet who wrote (Isaiah

55:12): "You will go out with joy and be led forth in peace. The mountains and hills will break forth before you into singing and all the trees will clap their hands."

Don't you love that symphony to nature? That call for all of us to just get away, take a walk in the woods, and look at all the trees that God made for us?

Go ahead, enjoy it. And feel God's smile.

3

Can You Make a Gratitude List?

The woman was almost ashamed when she whispered the question to me, "Do you sometimes feel far away from God, like he's not there?"

"Of course," I said.

She stared at me. "Really?" she asked, and her voice said something else. It was relief, knowing that she wasn't the only one.

"I was feeling kind of guilty about it," she said.

I told her that it wasn't as if she had stolen money from the collection plate. She was just feeling distant from God.

I sometimes feel distant from God.

Everyone has times when they feel distant from God, at least if they're being honest to God about it.

Or as a Catholic friend once told me, "I just went through a Doubting Thomas period."

She meant the Apostle Thomas, who was not with the others when the risen Jesus appeared to them after his Resurrection. They told Thomas about the miracle; about Jesus coming back from the dead. Thomas refused to believe it. In John 20:24–31, Thomas uttered the words that would later haunt him, "Unless I see the nail marks in his hands and put my finger where the nails were, and put my hand into his side [where he was speared], I will not believe it."

Poor Thomas has been savaged in sermons for centuries for simply saying what many of us have thought, "Look, you may be experiencing God right now. It may be great for you, but I'm not seeing or feeling anything."

A lot of us don't know how we should feel about God; we just know that we're missing something. This is not a major theological crisis, where we wonder if there even is a God or where God was when a child died, for example. It's not as if we're angry with God, or that we've lost faith in prayer. We still know God is there, and we believe he cares about us.

But not much is happening.

It's more like a slump, the everyday spiritual blahs. It's like biting into a piece of frozen pizza. You can still eat it, but you don't feel like you're getting much out of it.

It can happen in church. You look around and it seems everyone has more faith than you. They seem to sing louder, pray with more heart, and react more enthusiastically to the sermon. They seem to be cheering for God, letting the world know how God has blessed them and changed their lives. In some places, people in the pews raise their arms and shout like it's a football game. In other churches, they quietly kneel, heads bowed, connecting with God in silence.

I have been to both types of worship services, and found both spiritually fulfilling—or rather empty. In most cases, it wasn't the service, the music, the sermon. It wasn't even the grouch you invariably find in a pew near you.

It was me.

I was just like the woman confiding to me about her prayers seeming short, dry, and lost in spiritual space.

The temptation is to think we're alone on a spiritual journey that has hit a dead end in a dark alley. We don't know where to turn.

And the last thing we want to do is tell anyone about it.

One of the great revelations of reading the Bible is how every historical giant of faith seemed to have had periods of feeling like a spiritual midget. Peter is considered one of the fathers of the early Christian church, a close friend of Jesus. It was Jesus who told Peter that he would be a rock upon which the new church would be built. But when Jesus was arrested and headed to his execution, Peter wimped out and denied knowing Jesus *three* times, including once to a teenaged girl. It was the same Peter who told Jesus that he'd be there forever with his friend. The same Peter who pulled out a sword and cut off a man's ear when the soldiers came to arrest Jesus.

This same Peter lost faith, ran far from God.

I never blamed him for that.

The man was scared. His dreams seemed to be put to death with Jesus on that cross. He probably wondered if he just wasted three years of his life following Jesus around, three years when he could have made more money in the family fishing business. He had to wonder about his own faith, his own connection to God.

I think of another story about Peter, one where he usually gets a bad rap just like the maligned Doubting Thomas. In this account, Peter and the other disciples are in a boat. The water has turned ugly. A storm has made them panic. It must have been bad, because some of these guys were fishermen and used to being on the water.

Amid the thunder and wind and waves, Jesus appeared, walking on the water. Peter recognized him.

In Matthew 14:22–36, Jesus asked Peter to join him on the water. Peter left the boat, did very well until he was distracted by the storm, and then started to sink.

Peter screamed, "Lord, save me."

Jesus reached out, pulled Peter up, and said, "You of little faith, why did you doubt?"

Usually when this is discussed, we hear about Peter's lack of faith—how, if he only trusted God more, everything would have been okay. Then we're told that we need to keep our eye on God or else we will sink, too. We just need more faith.

It can become a guilt trip.

But as I read this story, I admire Peter. At least he had guts enough to get out of the boat and try to reach God. The other eleven just watched. They weren't willing to risk looking stu-

pid to get to God. So what if Peter became afraid in the midst
of a storm while walking on water? I'd probably have felt the
same way.

I sometimes think about Peter when I'm at church and everyone but me seems very locked into what is happening. I
think that if I just get out of my boat of doubt, take a few steps
on the water, and see what happens, I'll sing with everyone
else. I'll say the prayers out loud even if I really don't feel
like it. I'll tell myself that if I can just go with the flow, maybe
some of the spiritual juices will begin to bubble up.

Sometimes it helps; sometimes it doesn't.

Sometimes we feel like we're walking on water and sometimes we know we're sinking.

Sometimes, we need to tell someone how we feel, someone
who is smart enough not to take those doubts and turn them
into guilt. And then let that person just listen and pray with
us, reassuring us that God still cares even when it seems he's
on vacation.

Akron rabbi David Lipper told me, "God is still there, but
we're on the move."

Or, as someone else said, "If the devil can't make you sin,
he'll make you too busy."

Ain't that the truth?

Rabbi Lipper told me, "I go into a room, shut the lights,
close my eyes, and wait in the dark and the silence for God to
come. It's only then that I can begin to hear from God."

I've tried it and it's hard. Just sitting in the dark doing
nothing but waiting on God sometimes leads to more doubt,
more guilt. I feel as if I'm not doing it right, or I would *feel* or
hear something. Yet I do know that has worked for others. My
guess is that I never really gave this enough time.

"When I'm in those dry periods, I pull out my gratitude
list," said Bob Coombs, pastor of Grace Church in Norton,
Ohio.

Coombs said that when he makes lists of all the times God

has blessed him, all the times when God pulled him out of some mess, he begins to feel closer to God. It's just like a relationship. Want to feel better about a friend, a spouse, a relative? Think of everything good that that person has ever done for you.

Coombs also said we should quit beating ourselves up for not being as "spiritual" as someone else, or as connected with God as we should be. He said if we get into "the spirit of gratitude," the spirit of God often follows. Prayer is not an ATM machine. We don't just hit a few buttons and get what we want.

I really like the idea of the gratitude list.

I need to be reminded that I was born into a family with two parents who loved me. I was given a chance at solid education by those parents who valued education. I was given the ability to write, and a couple of enormous breaks early in my career that allowed me to publish books and reach major papers while still in my early twenties. I was given so much, and I'm still blessed so much. I have wonderful health. I have a super wife. I work for a good boss and a superb newspaper. I have never really been poor or hungry. I have friends who have stuck by me during some tough stages of my life when I was no bargain to be around.

I came to faith in Jesus Christ at a point in my life when I was discouraged, riddled with doubt, and spiritually empty. I was given forgiveness when I needed it most. I can think of times when God protected me from myself, when I did things that could have been very embarrassing had they become public. And I bet most of us can give thanks for similar things, because many of us have embarrassed ourselves and we know it could have been much worse.

Psalm 118 ends "You are my God, and I will give you thanks. . . . Give thanks to the Lord for he is God, his love endures forever."

When I want to get close to God, I do the same things that

make me feel close to my wife. I give thanks for God simply being there, for sticking by me and giving me second chances. My wife has done the same. And when I put my gratitude list down on paper, my heart does change.

God comes closer as my heart grows more grateful.

4

Why Me?

I don't want to deal with this.

That was my reaction when my father had his stroke. It was September 1993. My wife and I were on vacation in South Dakota when the call came from my aunt. My father was in a Florida hospital with what appeared to be a serious stroke.

My first thought was "It can't be that bad."

My second thought was "We just started vacation."

My third thought was "Let my brother take care of it. He lives in the same town as my father. Dad had just been in Ohio all summer and I spent a lot of time with him. It's my brother's turn."

I didn't know much about strokes. From a conversation with my brother, I learned that my father's condition had "stabilized." I learned that he was paralyzed on the right side and he couldn't really speak. I learned that the doctors were not optimistic about a full recovery, but they said they'd know more in a few weeks.

My mother had been dead since 1984, so I knew it would be up to my brother and me to handle this situation.

My father was always the strong one, a former minor league baseball player and a big man for his era—about six foot one and 190 pounds. He played center on his high school basketball team and for his army team during World War II. He was a mountain of a man to me, with a bald head, wide shoulders, a round belly, and strong arms. I remember him hoisting me up on those shoulders when was I young and we went to the old Cleveland Stadium. He held me up so high my head seemed to be in the clouds as we walked down the West Third Street Bridge to the games. From my father's shoulders, I could see the revolving Chief Wahoo sign on top of the stadium. I could see the deep blue of Lake Erie and the white sailboats on the waves. I felt like I could see the whole world from his shoulders. My father was always there to carry me.

Even as an adult, I never imagined a time when I'd have to carry my father.

This was the time. Down deep, I knew it.

Down deep, I knew I should end my vacation and fly to my father's side.

Down deep, I knew that's what he would do.

But I didn't.

I talked to my brother for a while, shaping the conversation so that I could hear what I wanted, namely, I could stay on vacation. There was nothing I could do in Florida. Maybe all of this would just go away in a few days. I had been closer to my father in the previous few years and had taken care of some minor things for him. It was about time my brother handled some things.

Over and over I told myself that. I passed the burden to my brother, while at the same time telling myself that it wasn't much to carry. Dad is in the hospital. The doctors and nurses are there. What could anyone really do?

Then I called my father-in-law, Dr. Robert Monroe. I told him about my father's stroke, and the symptoms.

"That sounds bad," he said.

I didn't want to hear that.

Dr. Monroe told me about a friend of his who had had a stroke several years before. The man was confined to a wheelchair. He could speak only a few words. He was in diapers. He needed twenty-four-hour care. He could live that way for a long, long time.

I *really* didn't want to hear that.

I knew I should go to Florida. Now. I know it was the Holy

Spirit speaking softly to me, over and over. The message was a whisper, but it was clear: "Just go."

At this point in my life, I had a dose of religion. I went to church most Sundays the same way most of us brush our teeth or use deodorant, just so we don't stink. But there was no heart behind it, no thought that I could connect with God and develop an Everyday Faith that would influence my life.

Instead of listening to what I know now is God's voice, I went from the Black Hills of South Dakota to the Badlands of North Dakota, another 350 miles away. My wife thought I should go to be with my father, but said little. My guess is she thought I needed to work this out my own way. I was emotionally numb.

I felt nothing —not good, not bad, not even worried. I felt like I was watching myself in a movie, and I wasn't doing much of anything but driving. When I did talk, it was about anything except my father's condition. I called my brother a few times and learned nothing much had changed. My father was bedridden. He couldn't speak. He was paralyzed. We needed to start thinking about rehabilitation centers, long-term care.

Two days later I finally started the drive back from the Dakotas to Akron, where I'd catch a plane to Florida. I stopped at a place called Burns Brothers Truck Stop outside of Mitchell, South Dakota. I tried to reach my brother, who was at the hospital in my father's room. He handed the phone to my father.

"Dad," I said. "This is Terry."

"Man," he said.

"Dad, how are you?"

"Man, MAN, MAN!" he said, and I could hear his voice cracking.

"Dad," I said. "I'll be there as soon as I can."

"Man," he said, weeping.

"I'll pray for you," I said.

I said that even though I really didn't pray much back then. About all I'd do was say, "God, help my father." I didn't know if God heard prayers. If God did, I wasn't sure how much, if any, attention God gave to what someone told me were "our little problems." I said I'd pray for people because that seemed like something I should say, not that I had any real plan to do it.

As I drove home, I thought about my father's condition. I thought about my reaction. I thought about how I had heard the voice to go and be with him, and how I had ignored it. I thought about how my father had taken me to games, played catch with me in the backyard. I thought of how my first job was at the food warehouse where he worked for years, and how I learned that my father was enormously respected. I thought about how it was time to be a real son, to care about someone besides myself, my career, and my bank account.

I also remembered Jesus saying we all had to carry a cross.

Guess this was my cross.

Actually, it was my father's cross.

My father was the one whose life was turned upside down and nearly destroyed. He was the one who could no longer dress himself, no longer cut his own food. He could no longer drive, no longer do much of anything besides sit in his favorite chair and watch TV, or play his favorite card game with his friends. He was the one in diapers, who needed help to go to the bathroom.

He was the one who felt trapped in a body that seemingly had died and betrayed him. He was the one who couldn't even be left alone in the house, who felt like a little kid. He was the one who had a million words running through his head, yet could speak only a few. He was the one who endured speech teacher and after speech teacher, therapist after therapist, without any major improvement.

He was the one who silently called out to God, wondering why this had happened to him.

Now, more than ten years from the day of my father's stroke, I can see how my trials with him were more like inconveniences compared to what my father endured.

While I was screaming in my head, "God, this isn't fair," it was my father who really had the right to feel that way. I still had my health, my freedom, my job, my wife, my friends. He had lost nearly all of that.

I was like a biblical character named Simon.

According to Mark 15:21: "A certain man from Cyrene, Simon, the father of Alexander and Rufus, was passing by on his way from the country and they forced him to carry the cross."

Simon happened to be coming to town when Jesus was being crucified. It was Roman tradition for a criminal to carry his own cross to the hill where the criminal was to die. But Jesus had been whipped and beaten so savagely, he crumpled to the ground and couldn't walk. So the Romans pulled Simon out of the crowd and said, "You carry this guy's cross." Simon had no choice. If he objected, they'd have said, "Fine, you can carry your own cross, and we'll crucify you, too."

The only other reference to this Simon is in Luke 23:26: "As they led him away, they seized Simon of Cyrene, who was on his way in from the country, and they put a cross on him and made him carry it behind Jesus."

That's all we know about Simon, who obviously didn't volunteer for duty.

My brother and I didn't sign up for what became a nearly five-year ordeal taking care of my father. We were like Simon, heading somewhere else, pulled out of a crowd and drafted into service. The job was nasty, and it came with very little reward.

Those early Christian writers should have told us more about Simon and given him more credit for what he did.

Instead, he gets two sentences, one each from Luke and Mark.

When we're called to be a Simon, it's usually for a miserable job with minimal rewards.

If you've ever had to raise someone else's child, you know the feeling. If you've ever had someone close to you become disabled, you know the feeling. If you did all the work on a project and someone else got the credit and the promotion, you know the feeling. If you ever stepped in to help someone and were hurt or betrayed, you know the feeling. If you've ever spent time with a loved one who has Alzheimer's and no longer recognizes you, then you know the feeling.

I have an excellent study Bible with thousands of notes for nearly every verse. It supplies lots of details, historical context, and analysis.

What does this 2,504-page book have to say about Simon of Cyrene?

"Colonies of Jews existed outside of Judea. Simon had made a Passover pilgrimage to Jerusalem all the way from Cyrene in North Africa. His sons, Alexander and Rufus, are mentioned here because they became well known later in the early church."

That's it?

I have some African American friends who mentioned how Simon ended up carrying the cross because he was dark-skinned, being from North Africa. That could be true. But you would think the scholars would tell us more about Simon, or at least talk about how this day affected him. His sons became important people in the early Christian church. Don't you think that seeing their dad carrying the cross and being a part of the crucifixion changed their lives?

Proverbs 16:9 reads: "A man plans his course, but the Lord determines his steps."

Simon thought he was going to town for a service at the temple, and ended up taking part in an event that changed history for millions of people over thousands of years. Simon had no idea that would happen, nor did he have much choice. He just did as he was told.

Being a Simon can change the lives of families. I doubt I would have become as serious about my faith without having been a Simon to my father.

Most of our lives are changed through trials and crises. Instead of asking "Why me?" we can become better people by becoming a Simon and accepting others' crosses.

5

Do You Remember Answered Prayers?

God does answer prayers, this I know, and not just because the Bible tells me so.

Why don't I appreciate that more? Why don't I keep track? Why am I more likely to remember the unanswered prayers? Why do I sometimes get stuck on the question of why some prayers are answered, while others seemed to be ignored?

I know, God answers every prayer.

Sometimes the answer is "Yes."

Sometimes the answer is "No."

Sometimes the answer is "Not Yet."

Don't ask me to explain it. And don't believe anyone who claims to have all the answers about prayer.

Don't you think there must be some mystery involved when we pray to a heavenly, invisible God about something that seems to be an impossible situation?

So prayer is weird, and we should just admit it. It also can bring up some tricky theological questions, such as "If God knows everything that happened and is going to happen, why should we bother to pray?"

A friend told me that he went through a period when that question spiritually froze him. He had a crisis in his business. His wife filed for divorce. He was in a helpless situation. He loved the Bible, prayed daily, but just lost faith—not in God, but in prayer.

He told me that he'd forgotten all his answered prayers. He was stuck on the prayers that seemed to go nowhere. He said he wrote a letter to a famous preacher whom he had met a few times. He didn't think the man would remember his name, but the man answered the letter.

"He basically reminded me that I'm not the first one to go through hard times," my friend said. "He wrote about others who suffered in the Bible. He reminded me that God didn't just bring me this far to forget me."

My friend said the letter was mostly tough love, a reminder that we all owe our next breath to God. At first, the letter upset him. It didn't seem very compassionate. But days later, it began to speak to him. He realized he was quick to accept all God's blessings, but not willing to deal with hard times.

My friend remembered that God clearly wants a relationship with us. He wants us to pray. Every great woman and man of the Bible had some type of prayer life. Christians believe Jesus was the Son of God, and part of the Blessed Trinity. He walked the earth as God. Yet he prayed to God the Father. Prayer was important to Jesus, and he had supernatural powers and insights.

There are biblical examples of Moses and Abraham engaging in what seem to be negotiations with God. Moses didn't want to follow God's orders and confront the Pharaoh, a truly twisted dictator. Moses told God that he was a lousy speaker and that he never wanted the job. God agreed to send his brother Aaron along with him to see the pharaoh. Aaron was a superior communicator. God heard Moses' pleas and responded during the forty years the Jews wandered through the wilderness. Moses asked for food, and manna rained down. He asked for water, and it came from a rock. Abraham begged God to spare the towns of Sodom and Gomorrah, asking whether God would show mercy if Abraham could find fifty good people, then forty, then twenty, then ten. It's as if Abraham was dealing with the great Car Salesman in the Sky, trying to get a good deal. This is not meant to be disrespectful, just to point out that prayer and a relationship with an unseen God is strange business, regardless of the power of your faith.

Jesus spent much of his ministry in prayer. The night before his crucifixion, he begged God the Father three times to "take away the cup," the execution that he knew he'd soon have to "drink."

It may sound simplistic, but I've decided that since every person of God prays to God . . . well, then I'm gonna pray.

I'm gonna pray even when I don't know if it will do any good. I'm gonna pray even when it feels like God is not listening. I'm gonna pray even when I'm not sure how to pray, and I'm gonna pray even when I don't feel like it.

In James 5:16 it says, "The prayers of the righteous are powerful and effective."

Does that mean God won't listen to the prayers of someone who is a spiritual mess? That doesn't seem to be the case because Jesus had tremendous compassion for the worst sinners who came to him with a sincere heart. Maybe it means if prayers are righteous they come from the right motives and are offered for the right reasons.

The Book of Psalms is 150 prayers, most written by King David. If you read them closely, it appears that many were composed during sleepless nights when danger and depression seemed ready to knock down David's door. Psalm 10 begins: "Why O Lord do you stand far off? Why do you hide yourself in time of trouble?"

David talks about how his enemies are out to get him. He begs God to protect him, at one point writing, "Break the arm of the wicked and evil man." He does this after reminding God, "You are a helper to the fatherless."

Scholars aren't sure what dire situation was occurring when David wrote this, partly because he had so many in his life. But it's obvious the prayer was answered because he wrote more psalms. We don't know if arms were broken, but he escaped.

Luke 6:12–13 says, "Jesus went out to a mountaintop to pray, and spent the night praying to God. When morning came, he called the disciples together and chose 12, whom he designated apostles."

Jesus prayed for guidance, so I pray for guidance. I'm not making any great claims about being some type of prayer warrior. It doesn't take long for my mind to wander. It doesn't take long for me to doubt what I'm doing. It doesn't take long for me to forget when my prayers are answered.

Which is really the point I want to make: Why am I surprised when God answers one of my prayers? And why do I soon forget the prayer that was answered?

If this sounds like a contradiction, so be it.

I find it easier to think about unanswered prayers. For years, my wife has battled severe allergies. We've often prayed about this situation. God has not changed her condition, although the allergies are under better control than when we first started praying. It's no miracle and I wonder why my wife—the best person I know—has to carry that burden.

Yet, my wife and I have probably had hundreds of prayers answered, if we had ever bothered to keep track. We prayed for her sister's situation as she took care of her dying husband—and something nearly miraculous happened to take away much financial strain. We prayed for a friend to get serious about her faith—did so for years—and it happened. We prayed for sick friends, we prayed for new jobs for other friends, and many times, the prayers were answered.

Would they have been answered had we not prayed? What impact did the prayers have? Does God need us to call attention to a situation before there is divine intervention? I have no idea how to answer those questions.

I do know that for prayers to mean more to me, I need to

treat prayers with more importance. I need to try to keep a record, much as I do with financial dealings and other parts of my life. Pastor Ronald Fowler of Akron's Arlington Church of God has started putting his prayer requests on index cards. Then he tapes the cards to a wall. When the prayers are answered, he puts a star on them.

After a while, the cards cry out about answered prayers. The record is there.

We might discover that we were praying for the wrong thing, and we should take a card off the wall. Or maybe some prayers just don't get answered, and we'll never know why.

But keeping track often shows that God answers more prayers than we think, and, often, in better ways than we asked for. Just staring at a wall of answered prayers is enough to lift our faith, and keep us praying even when we don't feel like it or fully understand how it works.

6

Be Still

His voice on the phone answering machine sounded desperate because it sounded so quiet, so calm, and so distant. It sounded like something from a computer, one of those voices telling you to watch out because you're almost at the top of the escalator.

It sounded like the voice of a dead man.

The voice belonged to a friend, but not a close one. I had known him for a few years. Most of our contact had been by phone—a conversation every few months. He worked in a social service field. We had an interest in prison ministry, and we were about the same age. He had been struggling with his job, with his marriage, with a nagging doubt that maybe he wasn't doing the right thing with his life; maybe he had missed God's call.

More than a few times he told me, "I'm just hanging on."

After a few of these conversations, I figured that he really didn't want me to do much but listen and encourage him. Besides, what could I do about his enormous problems? I couldn't fix his marriage. I couldn't change the structure of his job. I couldn't tell him what he was supposed to do with his life.

I wanted to take a shot at some of those problems. But really, what could I tell him that he didn't already know? He had more formal training in counseling and psychology that I did. In fact, he was supposed to know all the answers.

So I spent time listening, which is not one of my strengths.

I tried to tell him that he had a "good heart," that he really did care about others, and I knew that that was true. He had worked with an inmate from one of my Bible studies. It was years ago. The inmate was a young man who had grown up in chaos, drifted into drinking and crack, and seemed to stagger through life with the curtains drawn, the lights out. A desk had more personality than this inmate. He would not talk. He would look at you. He was not a bad person, just incredibly wounded and withdrawn. I had quit dealing with this inmate, but my friend stuck with him and continued to visit the inmate in different jails over the years.

When my friend told me he felt that he wasn't measuring up, I knew he didn't need a pep talk about the virtues of hard work. That was especially true when he told me about the history of his position, how he was the fifth person to hold it in the last fourteen years. Some quit, others were fired. All seemed overwhelmed. Given those facts, I kept telling him that he should stop beating himself up, that it sounded like he was doing as well as anyone ever had with a seemingly impossible job.

I became his cheerleader. He was not a needy guy. He called every three or four months. We may have seen each other once a year. I really didn't know that much about him when his disturbing message was left on my phone.

So I called him and he immediately said, "I just want you to know that I just got out of doing four days in detox."

That wasn't what I expected to hear, but I just mumbled, "Okay."

"I want to go back in," he said. "But they won't take me."

"Any drugs?" I asked.

"No, just drinking," he said.

"Sure?" I asked.

"Yes," he said. "I've been drinking since the seventh grade. I've had long stretches where I didn't drink, seven or eight years sometimes."

I suggested that we get together, that we meet at my church. He had met my pastor a few times and, as with most people who know the Reverend Ronald Fowler, there was instant respect.

"I'm not leaving the house," he said, his voice rising.

"If you've been drinking, that's okay," I said. "I'll pick you up and we'll go see him together."

"I'm not leaving the house," he repeated.

We talked a little more. Actually, I babbled and I realized he had tuned me out. He was fixated on two things: not leaving the house, and returning to the detox facility that had just released him.

"They won't take me back," he said. "I was just there in the afternoon. I begged. I pleaded. I cried. They said they couldn't take me back in. I wasn't drunk enough or something. My wife and kids have left. When they find out at my job, I'm finished."

During this admission, I was silently asking God, "Just what am I supposed to do? What if he tries to kill himself or something?" Rarely do I hear God's voice directly, and when I do, it's something short, like what I heard that night.

"Go to him," I heard. It was just a whisper.

I didn't want to do it. Actually, I wanted to go to my church that night to join my wife for a short prayer service and a chance to talk to people. I really believed that would have helped my friend. My church is the kind where you can bring almost anyone in any condition, and someone will help and pray for the person. There will be someone who will say, "Hey, I was just as drunk and feeling just as dumb and I know God wasn't done with me and he ain't done with you."

But that was *my* plan. And I was getting angry that my sometime friend couldn't see the wisdom in it. I was just trying to help, and this guy wouldn't listen. He just wanted to sit home and drink and feel sorry for himself.

A few years ago I would have told him exactly that. I would

have attacked him, because that was my style in a crisis: take command, issue orders, and develop a plan. If no one else had an idea, I would come up with one. And that's still my first instinct, as my wife and friends can tell you.

But this time, I heard, "Go to him."

And do what?

I don't drink. I don't like to be around people who are drunk. I don't know what to do in those circumstances.

I wondered why he called me. We weren't that close; I didn't even know where he lived. Why didn't he take his troubles somewhere else? I just wanted to be a good guy, meet my wife at church, and be all spiritual. What was wrong with that?

Then I thought of the famous parable of the Good Samaritan that Jesus told in Luke, in chapter 10. Two religious types don't stop to help a man who is beaten because they are on their way elsewhere, perhaps to a religious function. The man with no religious training is the one who takes time to help.

Sometimes I'm glad when I remember different Bible verses and stories because they keep me out of trouble. Other times, I hate it, because they remind me to do what God wants, not what I want. They force me to get my hands dirty with someone else's mess. I've been through enough to know these situations usually take more time than I want to spend.

In this case, I didn't want to spend any time on my friend's crisis.

Then I thought how my friend had visited that inmate. I knew of another family that he had helped, one struck by cancer that killed the husband and nearly took the life of the wife. And I knew if I had called him, he'd be there.

I didn't go to him because I'm some kind of saint; I went as much out of guilt as anything. I went a little resentful because it was not what I wanted to do that night. I went telling God, "You'd better help me with this, because I sure don't know what to do. It's your idea, not mine."

While that wasn't exactly my prayer, it was exactly my attitude.

So I asked my friend for directions to his house. He fought me for a while about coming, but I could tell that he wanted me there.

When I arrived, he met me at the door. He was not as drunk as I'd imagined. He had been crying earlier, but now was in a detached state. He led me to the living room. He sat in one chair and I sat across from him on the sofa. He didn't say much.

I stared at him and thought, "Now what?"

Finally, I said, "Have you eaten anything?"

He shook his head "no."

"When was the last time you ate?" I asked.

"I don't know," he said.

"Today?" I asked.

He shrugged.

I realized this was ridiculous, that I was acting like someone's grandmother who thought everything could be fixed with some chicken soup, pot roast, and a slice of cherry pie.

"All right, God," I prayed. "Now what?"

"Just shut up," I heard a whisper.

So I sat there. And he sat there. And no one said anything for a few minutes, which seemed like an hour.

Finally, he told me about the time in detox.

"I told the people about what I did for a living," he said. "They were a little surprised, but none really looked down on me. After a few days, they started coming to me for counseling. And I prayed with them."

He stopped.

I started to say something, but he interrupted.

"They wouldn't let me back," he said.

I talked about other detox places and said I'd be glad to drive him to any of them.

"*I don't want to leave the house,*" he said, his voice raised.

That's when I thought of another Bible story in the book of Job. Job had lost everything: his ten children, his wealth, and everything else had been wiped out. His wife said, "Why don't you curse God and die?" His body was being eaten away by worms and oozing sores. He was in utter despair.

My friend would never compare himself to Job. He knew his closet drinking had led to his family leaving him, and that his insecurity hurt his job performance. While he wasn't in much physical pain, his mental anguish was Job-like. He told me that he had thought of suicide, and I mentioned that was the one thing he couldn't do because it was a curse on families and it seemed to spread from one generation to the next. He knew that was true. His training made him more aware of the research and consequences than anything I could say.

"That's the one thing I won't do," he said. "That, I promise you."

Silence dropped on the room. It hung heavy. I had no idea what else to say. Then I remembered that during his suffering three of Job's friends showed up to comfort him, and the best thing they did was just sit there. When they began to speak, to play amateur theologians and psychologists, it just made everything worse. According to one Jewish tradition, no one is to speak until a mourner does. It's a great idea for all of us when we encounter hurting people.

So I kept quiet.

Finally, my friend asked me about my wife.

I talked about her, and told him how her music and singing had grown in our church. He said he'd never heard Roberta sing, and I thought about how her music has a soothing affect on most people. She sings a cappella, without music. She has sung for people right over the phone.

"What if I call her and she sings for you?" I asked.

He shrugged. He didn't seem to care much either way.

I called Roberta, explained the situation, and handed the phone to my friend. She sang a song that began, "I'm goin' through a storm, and I feel I'm by myself. No shoulder to cry on, Lord, I need your help . . . "

My friend began to cry as he pressed the phone closer to his ear. When Roberta was finished, he thanked her several times. Then he thanked me for calling her.

We sat quietly again. It was hard for me to keep my mouth shut. Then the doorbell rang and another friend arrived. He tried to convince my friend to go to the hospital, or another detox center.

"*I'm not leaving the house*," he said.

I had never met this new person before so we made a little small talk. Then the man said, "I'll stay with him, you can go. I'm his landlord. He's a good guy. I'll stay."

The three of us held hands and prayed. My friend could barely say anything, but silent tears rolled down his cheeks as I left.

The next day I called my friend. He said that he felt God's presence in the two of us who visited him. He said he was ready to go back into detox, wherever he could get in. He said he was glad his problem was "out of the darkness; no more secrets about me." He thanked me for "not coming down hard" on him.

I prayed with him on the phone.

The next day his landlord called me. My friend had gone back into detox and, through some rather amazing circumstances, ended up at the original treatment center. The landlord had driven him there.

"I just waited until he said he was ready to go," the landlord said.

Waiting quietly. That's something I'm still learning.

Can God Be a Father?

Most of us have heard the prayer that begins, "Our Father, who art in heaven . . ."

It's a prayer known as the Our Father, and many of us learned it as children. But some of us hear those words and think, "If God is like my father, I don't want any part of him."

When you hear some people tell their father stories, who can blame them for rejecting God as father?

Their fathers abandoned them. Their fathers beat their mothers, but made sure never to hit the face so no one would see the bruises. Their fathers sexually abused some of the children. Their fathers were cold, distant, utterly uninterested in the lives of their children. Their fathers pushed them, expected performance as a way to receive love—and they never seemed satisfied.

Our Father in heaven? Not a great image for many people.

Some biblical teachings just don't resonate with some people. In Luke 11:1–13, Jesus says, "Which of you fathers, if your son asks for a fish, will give him a snake instead? If he asks for an egg, will give him a scorpion?"

Some will read that and say, "Sounds like my dad. I needed a pat on the back and I got a boot to the behind."

Or they will remember, "We needed food and rent money, and the old man gambled most of it away. The rest, he drank up."

Or they think, "I have no idea what that means, I never had a father to give me anything. He was just this stranger who showed up every few years for a day."

When I speak in prison each week, one of my favorite biblical passages is Hebrews 12:7–10. It begins, "Endure hardship as discipline, God is treating you as sons. For what son is not disciplined by his father? . . . Moreover, we've all had human fathers who disciplined us and we respected them for it. . . . Our fathers disciplined us for a little while as they thought best, but God disciplines us for our own good."

I stop right there and say, "Some of you were disciplined by your fathers; they just beat you. Or the fathers just left you. Some of us have to realize that God is *not* like our fathers at all. Sometimes God has to step in and use anything from hardship to jail to teach us the lessons that we should have learned from our own fathers."

The point I try to explain to the inmates comes later in Hebrews 12:11: "No discipline seems pleasant at the time, but painful. Later on, however, it produces a harvest of righteousness and peace for those who are trained by it."

When I minister in jail, I emphasize to the inmates that God is allowing turmoil in their lives to get their attention. He wants to bring some order, some discipline, and some time for learning the right way—something too many fathers fail to teach their children.

Inmates like to receive cards to send out on Mother's Day. They all seem to have some woman they love, be it their biological mothers, grandmothers, aunts, or just someone who stepped in and loved them unconditionally. But on Father's Day, few inmates want cards because no one in their lives is worthy of being honored on that day.

For many, Father's Day is almost like a day of mourning. What is there to celebrate? The pain of a missing father? The hole in the heart from a father who held back his love? Yet, this topic is ignored by many religious leaders who ignore the pain that people have in their hearts when it comes to the subject of fatherhood.

Clerics sometimes stand in their pulpits and talk about God

as a father, believing that will help people get to better know God. Instead, it drives them away.

Even the best fathers can still fall short of the image of God. I was blessed with a terrific father, although I never really began to appreciate him until I was well into adulthood. That's when I began to hear father horror tales from friends. It's when I realized how much my father taught me about the value of hard work, about respecting others, about enjoying sports and staying away from drugs, alcohol, and people whose lives were chaos and wanted me to join them. My father was steady. He was always where he should have been. He always supported his family. You could count on my father to keep his word, and he expected you to do the same.

But my father was not hugger. He didn't offer much praise past a grunt and a quick nod. He expected performance and achievement, and he made me believe that was the way to gain his approval. I often felt that I fell short, as if he were hoping for just a little more from me. I intentionally used the word "felt," because it was just that, a feeling.

When I thought about God, I saw him the same way as I saw my father: steady, honest, strong, a quiet leader. But I also believed that I didn't quite measure up to God's standards. Of course, that's true. God is holy and God is perfect, so everyone falls short in some way. God loves us anyway. For me, that was difficult to accept. There are times when I still struggle to believe it.

Often, fatherhood takes a beating in the media. In TV shows and movies, Dad is sort of an overgrown, overmatched forty-something who's still acting like a teenager. These dads need their wives and kids to straighten them out. Some TV fathers are demented tyrants or religious zealots or womanizers who have no interest in children. When people with those pictures of fathers find themselves seeking God, hearing that God is like a father can cause them to turn off that spiritual channel.

When Jesus prayed he used the word, "Abba," which is like "Daddy." Jesus had a healthy relationship with God, one that we all could use with our father in heaven or on earth. Jesus had a serious level of respect and even a little awe, but the engine driving his relationship with his father was love.

My wife had a father who loved her, hugged her, and encouraged her. She says her father seemed a lot like Jesus to her because of his unconditional love for her. Her father still had standards and rules, but she never doubted that he loved her even when she knew she had let him down. For her, the idea of God the Father is comforting.

If that's true for you be very thankful.

In Psalm 2:7, David wrote, "[God] said to me, 'You are my son and today I have become your father.'"

As I read that verse, I thought of a friend who grew up in foster homes and never knew his father. After a period of petty crime and drug dealing and a heartbreaking divorce, he became a Christian and found a new life. He now has six children and a solid second marriage and is one of the people whom I admire tremendously.

We were talking about a mutual friend who had stepped in to father a child who was not his biological son. We saw this young man pulling a wagon, with the boy in the back. Both were laughing.

"Now that guy is a real hero," said my friend, the father of six.

So is my friend.

And both of these men are raising children who won't flinch when they hear the words "God the Father."

FAITH IN YOURSELF

8

Do We Really Want to Be Healed?

I don't like pain.

When I start to feel anything remotely like a headache, I take a couple of pills. When my stomach begins to bother me, I take another medicine. When I'm in a tough spot that demands a lot of hard work for little gain, my first inclination is to quit.

I pray, too.

Usually, it's something like "Lord, get me out of this!"

When I'm sick and exhausted, I know exactly what will make me feel better.

Rest . . . Go to bed early, sleep a little late.

Rest . . . Get off the phone, off the computer, off the treadmill of work.

Rest . . . That's what will do it, where the real healing will come. Call in sick. They can publish the paper without me for a couple of days.

Rest . . . Most things in life can wait. Most calls don't have to be answered today. Very few e-mails do. Even if I stop, the world will keep spinning and others will keep living. Nothing I have to do is really that important.

But here's the problem: I don't really want to rest. I don't want to shut down for a few days. I don't want to change. I don't even really want to be healed; I just want to feel better.

I want the shortcut, the quick fix. I want to keep feeding the side of me that is addicted to action. I love the pursuit of stories, the sheer delight that comes from writing, and the rush that is the result of seeing my stories published in the newspaper. So when I'm sick, I just want to get better so I can keep doing the things that I love doing even if some of those things are what wore me down and made me sick in the first place.

Maybe that's why I understand people who battle addictions.

I've been working in weekly jail ministry since 1998. Most of the inmates are hooked on crack cocaine, meth, and alcohol or prescription drugs. It's usually several things on that list, and other things most of us could never imagine. Inmates often come from dismal family backgrounds and are scarred by abuse, abandonment, and rejection. There is only one thing that frightens most of them more than staying in jail: it's leaving jail and trying to live differently.

Addiction is real. There are significant psychological and physical hammerlocks that it puts on the hearts and minds of the addicts.

But many will privately confess that the only thing worse than being on drugs is trying to figure out how to live without them. They've become used to days filled with figuring out how to get drugs and how to stay away from the police and angry, vengeful dealers. They are hooked on the adventure drugs—the excitement of the deal, the fear of being caught, the high that comes from scoring the dope and finally using it. They are like athletes getting ready for a game. They scout their opponents, scheming ways to beat him, and then revel in the victory.

Compared to that rush, going to school or working a construction job or at Wal-Mart seems boring. Many simply can't see themselves in a "normal" life, because life has never been normal. When life does seem to be going well for these inmates on the outside, a shocking number of them will take ridiculous risks that lead them back to jail. One deputy told me that he asked twenty-five inmates how many times they had been to jail. He wrote down all the numbers, and then computed the average. It was *seven*. The typical inmate had been in jail *seven times*, and that probably was a low estimate. Often, inmates lose count of their time because they've been jailed so often.

Many addicts are paralyzed like a man who Jesus found by a pool of water called Bethesda. It was where people would dump "the blind, the lame, the paralyzed," according to John 5:1–15.

Jesus found a man who had been paralyzed for thirty-eight years. He was on the ground, near a small pond. He was hopeless. No one helped him, no one paid attention to him, and he didn't believe anyone ever would. Very few of us have been paralyzed like the man in John's Gospel. But most of us know about rejection, about hopelessness, about feeling stuck. We have to be careful, because that sense of being a victim—even when it's true—can be addictive. And when someone or something comes along and presents the chance for real change and a new life that can be very scary.

Sometimes, we need to be clear about what we're asking God to do. Is it that we just want him to take away pain? Or do we just want to get through the day? Or do we want real change, a dramatic healing? A lot of us aren't sure, because change is frightening.

I went to Mexico City with the Cleveland Indians for an exhibition game in 1980. The team stayed at a Sheraton hotel, which was one of the best places in the city. On the sidewalk in front of the hotel was a line of beggars—blind, lame, paralyzed—along with women and infant children. Nearby was a group of older children. Sometimes their families would dump them at this spot in the morning, then pick them up at night, and take whatever money they had collected. Others just lived on the street, many in boxes or under bridges.

These people were different sizes and ages, but what they had in common was an appalling lack of teeth and clothes that were nothing more than rags. Shoes were stuffed with paper to cover holes. One older woman sat on a tattered rug rocking what I thought was a baby in her lap. A second look revealed it was a doll. I guessed that in her past a child had died, and she was emotionally scarred by it. She was a lost soul with a distant, unfocused stare; her eyes seemingly so dead they could no longer weep another tear.

All these people were begging for money, for food, or for attention. They fought for the best spots on the sidewalk. They screamed at each other in between their pleas to visitors for just a few coins, a candy bar, anything in your pocket. It was a scene of utter desperation.

People at the hotel told us that many of the beggars had been there for years. They also warned us that the beggars would fight each other if we gave one of them some money. And they told us that a few of the seemingly blind and lame were healthy; they just didn't want to work. I remember feeling overwhelmed and more than a little frightened as I walked past them. In fact, I almost jogged by them, making no eye contact and wanting to get quickly into the hotel.

Jesus might have encountered something like the beggars of Mexico City when he visited a place called the Sheep Gate. Jesus spotted one man who had been there the longest, a man whose only wish was to get into the pool of water, believing it would heal him.

Jesus said to the man, "Do you want to get well?"

The man said, "Sir, I have no one to help me into the pool when the water is stirred. While I am trying to get in, someone goes down ahead of me."

The man was so caught in the jaws of rejection, so trapped in a body that wouldn't move, that he didn't hear the question from Jesus. He was fixated on the pool, not listening to the one who could give him what the Bible calls living water and a new life.

What the man really wanted to do was complain to Jesus, and hope that maybe Jesus would carry him to the water. It was impossible for the man to picture a life where he could actually move on his own. His heart was in worse shape than his legs.

Rejection does that to us. It takes us so far down; we don't see a supernatural hand being extended to us. We've been praying for so long and heard nothing but the sad beating of our battered hearts. After a while, we assume no one is really listening. Novelist Irwin Shaw wrote a short story called "God Was Here but He Left Early." If you haven't ever had that feeling in your life, just wait, you will.

There are times when I really don't want things to change; I just want to complain. Or at least I don't want to do what is necessary for real healing. I'd rather whine about being sick and take pills than slow down for a day and let my body recover from the flu. I'd rather gulp my Diet Pepsi and complain about heartburn than spend a few days drinking water and cleaning out my system. I'd rather play the victim—at least in my own head—even if I don't complain to someone else about it. I just suck it up and move forward, chin out, and give myself credit for carrying the worries of the world on my back.

I'll bet there are times when that happens to you, too. Ever notice how easy it is to feel sorry for ourselves when we're not feeling well?

In the Bible story, Jesus saw a man stuck on self-pity. He didn't even touch the man. Instead, he simply ordered, "Get up! Pick up your mat and walk."

I can imagine Jesus screaming at the guy by the pool, trying to break through the mental wall of rejection, despair, and self-pity. It was like Jesus was saying, "There's hope. You can be healed. Get up and walk! DO IT NOW!" Jesus knew the man's pain was as much emotional as physical, that they were tied together and choking the man's soul.

The Apostle John writes, "At once, the man was cured. He picked up his mat and walked."

But the story doesn't end there. A while later, Jesus saw the man near the temple.

"See, you are well again," said Jesus. "Stop sinning, or something worse may happen to you."

When I first read it, the comment seemed so strange. Stop sinning? The guy was paralyzed for thirty-eight years! What could he have done? But Jesus was dealing with something much deeper than the man's physical and mental condition. He wanted the man to be able to walk spiritually, after being an emotional cripple for so long. The man had built up thirty-eight years' worth of resentment from watching people walk by, day after day. He had to have days where he seethed in anger over the rejection, and the envy that came from seeing other people able to walk and live regular lives while he was sentenced to a body that seemed to have died on him.

Rejection hurts.

Some of us hate to admit it. We say that we really didn't want that job, or we couldn't expect that parent to treat us with love and respect. Many of us deny there is any injury. We try to push our way through it. Quit whining and get on with life, we say. If we are scarred from rejection, so what? Everyone has scars. That's true, but we don't want to pick at the scars, opening old wounds and causing infection. We tend to do that late at night when we can't sleep, staring at the ceiling and going over and over the old conversations and slights. We may have overcome those setbacks, but the pain lingers. We wish we had said *this*—instead of *that*. We wish he hadn't said something else, and we wonder what they meant with that line about our personality. We say we have let it go, but down deep, we know otherwise.

After a while rejection ruins our relationship with others and with God.

We may be physically healed, but we remain emotional cripples.

Healing means change in our lives. It meant that the man

in the Bible story had to walk on his own, take responsibility for his own life. He could no longer wait for someone else to carry him to the water. In fact, he may be called to do the carrying.

So it is with some of us. We have to admit our hurt. We have to pray about it. We have to pray for the strength to live differently, to leave the scars to God and let him heal them. We have to go back to one of the basic building blocks of our faith: Life is not fair, and it never will be on this earth. But God does believe in us, sometimes even more than we believe in ourselves. God is in the business of healing, not just our bodies but also our heads and hearts.

I need to tell that to myself over and over. The newspaper doesn't make me into a workaholic. The reason I work too much is because I like the work. I understand the work, and I function well in that part of my life. It's why so many people become hooked on work. We learn what it takes to do a good job, and we understand the rewards and penalties. It makes more sense and is easier to comprehend than our personal lives, where families (especially children) can ambush us with demands and problems that seem overwhelming.

I prefer work to regular life. The newspaper is like many other businesses in that it operates every day. For a writer, the newspaper is like a starving monster bellowing, "Feed me words, feed me words!" I can write nearly every day, and the paper will be glad to publish what I write, assuming the quality is respectable. Writers have to fill space. I understand writing, and I like newspapers. I have been successful as a newspaper columnist, and it's tempting for me to write under stress.

One of the first things I did after learning of my father's death was to write a column about it. It was my way of coping and grieving, and it was a positive.

But there are times when I work too much, when I need to pay attention to things at home. And when I'm honest with myself, I know I didn't need to work that night my father died. It was not good for my marriage, my emotional health, or my spiritual life.

I promise and pray to cut back. I do, for a while. Then the temptation is there to go back to the old comfort zone.

Do I want to be healed?

It's a question every one of us needs to ask.

9

How Can I Serve?

Sometimes, churches really blow it.

When they want people to become involved, to serve God, they usually mention sharing faith with others. But not everyone is an evangelist. Some struggle to talk about their faith because it's difficult for them to talk about anything that's personal. They just don't communicate very well. They love to do things for others, not talk.

Dr. Gary Chapman wrote an excellent book called *The Five Love Languages*. His point is that we aren't all wired the same way; we relate differently. One of the "Love Languages" is called "Acts of Service."

People who don't have the confidence to talk about faith, love, or something else close to their hearts, may use the language of "service." They feel inadequate with strangers. But put them in the food kitchen where the poor are served, and they'll set up tables and chairs, then help make meals. They feel awkward and overmatched trying to talk to the people coming off the street, but they are content to clean up afterward. They'd be terrified if they had to teach a simple Sunday school class. But they could copy and pass out lesson plans, and make sure everyone had coffee or something to drink. Then they would put all the chairs back in place when class is over.

We need far more servants and followers than leaders and teachers. We need people who are willing to do the work that draws little notice, but is so needed. Those who are willing to cook meals, sweep floors, take out trash, and scrub toilets deserve to be praised, not made to feel inadequate because they don't want to lead or teach. They should feel good about being able to fix the heating system, paint the walls, or even change the oil in the car for someone who can't afford it.

Not everyone can be Billy Graham or Pope John Paul II, nor is that type of teaching a worthy goal for them.

Instead, these "acts of service" types should be encouraged to do what they enjoy and is their strength—and not dwell on their weaknesses.

Some churches put too much emphasis on leadership. They have seminars in how to lead, how to develop leaders, how to inspire others to become leaders. We all need leaders, but we need servants even more. The problem is that leaders naturally lead many churches.

Those giving sermons are people who are comfortable in front of groups. They find it easy to talk to fifty people or five hundred people. But put the talkers in a kitchen with five hungry people waiting for supper, or in the garage with a car that won't start, and you'll see panic. Suddenly, they wish they had the help of one of the "quiet" types who may not be good with people but sure know their way around a stove or an exhaust system.

The quiet types also may be in the choir. They'd rather cut their tongues out than sing solo. They don't think their voices are very strong, but they love being part of the group, singing in the chorus. They have no desire to pick the music or conduct the choir. They may like to pray for everyone involved in the service. They know church is not about them; it's about people coming together to praise and learn about God, and to help each other.

One of my favorite biblical characters is Andrew. When I was first studying Christianity, I concentrated on the apostles. I always thought Peter or John had to be the first to follow Jesus, especially Peter, the "rock" of the new church and the star of so many sermons.

But it was Andrew, the brother of Peter, who was first.

I've been in and out of churches much of my life, and I've never heard a single sermon about Andrew. I'm not even sure I've ever heard anything about him. But Andrew was in a crowd when Jesus spoke one day. Andrew's initial move wasn't to preach the message of Jesus to others.

The first thing Andrew did was find his brother Peter and tell him, "We have found the Messiah." Then, according to John 1:41, "he brought [Peter] to Jesus."

In the book of Matthew, Andrew and Peter were the first two disciples, followed by John and James.

What's the point?

We have no book of Andrew in the Bible. We know of no great sermons from Andrew, no miracles performed by Andrew, nothing about Andrew that seems especially remarkable. Not unless you happen to think a big faith, a small ego, and a willingness to serve are indications of spirituality. Not unless you take the words of Jesus to heart when he said he came not to be served, but to serve others. Not unless you realize that without Andrew, there probably would be no Peter who helped changed the course of history.

Peter was loud and opinionated. He probably talked enough for everyone in the family. Andrew was the silent sibling, the one who knew better than to try to compete with Peter for attention. So he kept his mouth shut, stayed in the background. He was content to be in the presence of Jesus, to try to get closer to God and to do the little things that seldom are noticed.

If Andrew worked at a food pantry for the poor today, you wouldn't find him leading the prayer before the meal or even handing out the meals. He'd be in the kitchen, peeling the potatoes. He would be the one who earlier had driven around to pick up food that was being donated. He would be the one later to wait until everyone was finished then help put together packages of leftovers to be given to the elderly to eat the next day. Andrew would clean up the kitchen. He'd be polite to people, but say little. He'd be the kind of person who seems like a good listener, who would have a way of letting everyone else talk and feel good just being in his presence.

There are Andrews everywhere, women and men. They never get their due, and they will say they really don't expect much praise. That's not why they serve. Yet, they should be praised. We need to notice them, to encourage them.

I've worked in food kitchens, and I can assure you we need far more people like Andrew than like Peter. I'm embarrassed as I write this, because I no longer do the Andrew-type work. When I volunteer at the local City Mission each month, I'm the Peter. I'm the one who speaks to people coming in at the chapel service before the meal. I'm the center of attention. And I confess that while I stop in the kitchen before the meal to find out what's for dinner (so I can tell those coming in), I rarely thank the volunteers. I'm just as guilty as church leaders who forget about those people needed to do the real work.

There's a terrific story in John 6:1–15. Jesus had been speaking to a crowd of five thousand, and they didn't want to leave when he was done with his message. They followed Jesus up a mountain. They had been outside for hours.

Jesus said to Philip, "Where shall we buy bread for these people to eat?"

Philip said they could work for eight months and not have enough money to feed everyone.

Andrew watched this, and then wandered off. He found a boy "with five small barley loaves and two small fish." He took the boy to Jesus. But even Andrew expressed some doubt as he said to Jesus, "How far will [the food] go among so many?"

Jesus took the loaves and fishes, prayed, and turned them into enough to feed the huge crowd, with twelve baskets left over, one for each apostle.

Sermons understandably focus on the miracle, but I like to focus on Andrew's faith. He didn't give his opinion about how to feed the people. He heard Jesus talking about feeding the hungry, so he looked for some food. He found the kid, but it would have been easy to think, "Five loaves, two crummy fish. Forget it."

Instead, he brought the boy to Jesus. He seemed to be thinking, "I don't know what to do with this, but maybe Jesus can figure something out. He's closer to God than I am."

Andrew did have doubts. He may have been afraid that the others would make fun of him, bringing a boy with so little, hoping that somehow it would feed thousands. Jesus took what Andrew brought and turned it into one of the most remarkable stories in the Bible. Andrew was smart enough to know that he had limits but that God could do something big with just a little faith.

Imagine the enormous courage it took for Andrew to invite his brother Peter to first hear Jesus. What if Peter thought Jesus was a fraud? Can you imagine how Peter would have ridiculed his brother? When Andrew wasn't sure what to do, he went to Jesus, with his brother, and with the boy with the loaves and fish. Then Andrew got out of the way and watched what God would do.

There's a brief mention of Andrew in John 12:20–22. It simply says some Greeks wanted to meet Jesus. They made the request to Philip, another apostle. Philip told Andrew, and both of them went to Jesus, who then spoke to the crowd.

That's all we know about Andrew from the gospels, but these are lessons from him. He wasn't afraid to invite people to meet Jesus. He didn't say much. He had no sales pitch, no magnetic personality. But if Andrew were around today, he'd invite friends to his church, to meet his minister or someone in the church whom he respected. He'd be very unassuming, and almost expect to be turned down. But he'd keep asking others. He would not be a pest. He would instinctively know that part of the reason some people give up on church is that no one has asked them to come back.

Andrew also is loyal. Dallas pastor Chuck Siwindoll once said, "Do you know that seventy-five percent of ministry is just consistently showing up?" That's what an Andrew understands. Just being there for others means so much.

I've spoken to different groups about Andrew, and the response is usually overwhelming, especially from women. They are the spine of many churches, doing the grunt work and rarely being noticed for it. There are men who serve as Andrews, as well. My church is in the inner city, and we have guys who are security guards in the parking lot during services. They also direct traffic.

My first little league coach was an Andrew. He didn't want to coach us, but when the regular coach quit someone had to do it. The new coach didn't know a lot about baseball, nor did he make claims of expertise. He simply made out the lineup card, tried to make sure everyone played a little bit in each game, and didn't seem especially upset if we lost. He knew Little League was about the kids, not him. He loved to take us out for ice cream after every game, win or lose.

Everyone knows an Andrew. You may have one in your family. There probably are more than a few at work, at school, at church, or somewhere else. When you see one, make sure to thank him or her. And if you are an Andrew, don't belittle what you do, because you mean more to God than you'll ever know.

10

Why Is It So Hard to Pray Out Loud?

Before I became serious about my faith, I talked to a pastor about some problems I had dealing with my father's stroke. The stroke caused so much pressure for me on every level, from money to emotions to marriage to career. When I finished, the man said he'd pray for me, and the meeting was over. I assumed the guy would keep his word, but I also believed the pastor was just going through the spiritual motions.

I told this story to a friend who was challenging me to read the Bible. My friend wanted me to take faith seriously and get to know God by studying the gospels of Luke and John.

"You mean that guy didn't even pray with you?" my friend asked.

No one had ever "prayed with me," unless a group all said a set prayer together.

"Let's pray now," my friend said.

He ran a small business. We were in his office and he shut the door. It was just the two of us. He knew the struggles I had with my father's situation. He took my hands—this seems strange—and he began talking as if God were in the room with us. That seemed even stranger. He talked about the mounting bills. He talked about the frustrating circumstances with doctors. He talked about my father's need for peace, and about all of us needing patience. He talked about other things that I can't remember right now. I just know that he seemed very secure talking to God. I had never heard a prayer like it, and it did give me a sense of peace. I told him that.

He said, "That's prayer: talking to God with respect, but also like you know God."

That was a breakthrough for me. The idea that I could talk to God about what was going on in my life surprised me. Most of my prayers my first forty years were memorized and mostly meaningless. When they came from the heart, they usually were something like "God, get me out of this mess! If you do, I'll be good! I promise!"

I'm no prayer expert. I still don't pray as much as I should. I find it easier to read a book about prayer than to actually pray.

Surveys show that about 80 percent of people say they pray at least once a week. I believe it. Or at least, we want to pray.

How many times have you heard someone say they'll pray for you? How many times have you said you would do the same? And how many times have you actually remembered to pray for that person? My batting average in this area would probably get me cut from any Little League team. Too many times I've had people ask me to pray for them and I said I would. What kind of heathen clod would I be if I said, "Nah, I don't have time—I'll probably just forget"?

But I often don't have time, or at least, I don't make time. And I certainly do forget to pray for people. Sometimes, I've even promised to pray for someone and fully intended to do so. But there are times when I've promised to pray for people just to shut them up. They are going into a very long, painful story. I know there is nothing tangible that I can do for them. Nor do I have the time (or patience) to listen. Perhaps I have heard some of their story before, and it's obvious from the start of the conversation that not much has changed. I don't want to hear it again.

"I really feel bad about that," I say. "I'll pray for you." Then, I'm gone.

"I'll pray for you" has been turned into a quick exit line.

As I write this, I realize that listening to someone's heartache is a form of prayer, especially when we actually pay attention and perhaps ask a few questions to prove it. For me, listening is harder than praying, and praying doesn't always come easy.

I realize that everyone is not like me. There are people who are dedicated to prayer. When they say they'll pray, they pray! They keep lists, and pray through the lists, naming each person and asking God to meet the need. They may even write little notes next to the person's name so they don't forget why they are praying.

I'm not one of these people.

I doubt some of you are those people. So what does it mean when we say, "I'll pray for you"?

It means absolutely nothing unless we pray.

Several years ago, I heard a sermon from a minister who admitted he had a terrible memory and sometimes struggled with prayer. He would promise to pray for someone, then forget totally, or remember the person but not the reason for the prayer.

"So I just started praying with people right on the spot," he said. He may take the person's hand and pray. Or perhaps touch his shoulder. Or just say, "Let's both close our eyes and let me pray for you." He didn't recite the entire book of Deuteronomy. He didn't go on and on. He didn't act like he invented prayer. He had, perhaps, just been told that someone was sick, so he talked to God about it.

Here's an example: "Father, my friend's mom has cancer. You know it's serious. You know that she and the family are frightened. You know they aren't sure what kind of treatment to use. I pray for guidance for the family, for the doctors and all the medical people as they consider what to do next. I pray for healing for her. I pray for comfort and peace as she endures this pain. I pray that you speak to her during this time.

I pray that the family stays together under this stress. I pray that something amazing happens. And I pray this in the name of Jesus."

That's my prayer, one that I just made up. But it's similar to what I've prayed for people in this kind of situation before.

You may think it's a good prayer or a bad prayer. Or you may think it's too long or too short. Or that I should have prayed for something else or in a different way.

It really doesn't matter what you think of my prayer. It's between God and me, and I trust God to sort it out. All I can promise is that it's a sincere prayer. And I believe that praying it out loud with someone in person gives it a special power. I promised to pray for someone and I did. That person knows I prayed, because he or she was there with me. And I hope they were praying, too, even if all they could do was add an "Amen" after I finished.

I've heard people say, "I'm just not comfortable praying out loud."

Wait a minute, I used to say that! But I've learned there's nothing "comfortable" about honest Everyday Faith. There is nothing comfortable about someone who has a father with Alzheimer's, a son in jail, a daughter on the verge of divorce, or a friend facing bankruptcy.

There was nothing comfortable about changing my father's diapers after he had a stroke, or cleaning up his bed each morning. But in its own demanding way, it brought me closer to my father and to God. Men like my father who grew up during the Depression and World War II understand better than most of us that life isn't meant to be comfortable, and that no one ever promised us that we would be happy.

When my friend prayed for me about my father his own business was in financial crisis. He survived it, but not before he went through a lot of personal pain. He had lost a brother in Vietnam, was shot himself in Vietnam, and later lost his twenty-two-year-old daughter to cancer.

Through it all, he kept praying even when his prayers were mostly tears.

I knew all this when he prayed with me, which is why it was so powerful. He didn't act like Moses coming down the mountain with the Ten Commandments; he was just one hurting guy praying with another.

From him, I learned to pray with people on the spot. But I also learned to do it discreetly. If prayer happens at a restaurant, don't stand on the chair and announce to everyone in the place, "Hey, my buddy Joe here has a porn problem, his marriage is falling apart, and he wants to kill himself. So let's all bow our heads while I lead us in prayer for his deliverance."

Take the guy aside, maybe to the parking lot. Sit in the car with him for a moment, put your hand on his shoulder, and pray. God doesn't judge our prayers by length or style points, just sincerity.

In Matthew 6:5–8 Jesus said, "Don't be like the hypocrites, for they love to pray standing in the synagogues and on street corners to be seen by men. . . . But when you pray, go into your room, close the door and pray to your Father. Then your Father who sees what is done in secret will reward you. And when you pray, do not keep on babbling like pagans, because they think they will be heard because of their many words. Do not be like them because your Father knows what you need before you ask him."

There are a lot of mysteries about prayer. I'm not sure what exactly is meant when Jesus says your Father "knows what you need before you ask him." My guess is God knows the situation, but he still wants us to talk to him about it. Just as we often know what's going on with someone whom we love, but we still want to hear from them.

Jesus was not against public prayer. He also said in Mat-

thew 18:20: "For where two or more come together in my
name, there I am with them."

That indicates we do need to pray together; and there is
something special about that kind of prayer. Just don't do it
to show off. And don't fall into one of those baritone prayer
voices where some people try to sound as if they *are* God, not
praying *to* him. Jesus was just saying, "Be yourself, because
God knows who you are anyway."

For years, I hated praying out loud. I thought I sounded
stupid. I wasn't sure what to say. I was sure that I was "doing
it wrong." But I stayed with it because down deep, I knew
it was the right thing to do. Now, I practice prayer. A friend
may tell me about a problem, and I'll e-mail him a short prayer
later on, assuming I believe it doesn't offend him. Or else, I'll
pray on the phone if the issue comes up in conversation.

I'll also ask my friend if he is okay praying on his end.
If not, I'll say, "Just let me pray for a minute, and you do it
silently." I once prayed about forty-five seconds for a woman
at a fast-food window. She was a single mom and was up for a
new job with better pay. A week later, I saw her and she said
she had been hired, and thanked me for the prayer. Not every
prayer is answered, but some of them are and it's great to celebrate when that happens.

Some people can pray up a tornado, others barely a trickle.
God hears every voice raised to him, as long as it's not one of
those "Bless us, Lord, and these thy gifts, pass the corn and
don't forget the fresh-caught fish."

There are times when people come to me with incredible,
overwhelming problems. I don't even know where to start
with prayer, so I'll just take their hands and say, "Lord, you
know this is a mess. You know all the pain that my friends are
feeling. You know what needs to happen here, I don't. So I
just call out to you to help the situation. Give us the strength
to trust you to deal with it in your way because it's obvious
that our way isn't working."

That's it, a prayer for something even if I really don't know what.

This kind of prayer is very biblical. In Romans, Paul writes, "In the same way, the [Holy] Spirit helps us in our weakness. We do not know what we ought to pray, but the Spirit intercedes for us with groans that words can't express."

Great revivals and church services are wonderful, but God can speak to us anywhere, anytime. And God expects us to do the same. For most of us, praying out loud isn't natural unless it's with a mob in church. Men especially struggle with prayer. I'm convinced that praying out loud with my wife Roberta is the cement that holds our twenty-eight-year marriage together, and neither of us came from denominational backgrounds where that kind of prayer was done. Our marriage and connecting with God and with each other is more important than any tradition.

We try to pray each morning, no matter if I'm home or traveling. We occasionally miss, and I find I regret it later in the day. We'll do it on the phone if I'm not at home. When I see that she's upset, I wait a few minutes for her to calm down and then suggest that we pray.

I'll say something like: "Father, I thank you for this great wife. She has been a tremendous blessing to me. You see how she is stressed. You know her battles. I pray for calm and clarity in this situation. I pray that you help me to help her, and help me to listen to her. I pray that your power stays in the middle of our marriage, and that I be the man that you want me to be."

As the Reverend David Loar from Fairlawn-West United Church of Christ said, "It's not about the head, it's about the heart. Men think prayer has to be done right. Our heads get in the way of real communication."

Guys, we need to work at prayer much as we would work at getting in shape. When your idea of exercise is sitting on the sofa doing arm curls with a can of Pepsi and a ham sandwich, those early trips to the gym are terrifying. Muscles ache. Sweat fills the eyes. The chest hurts. It seems like it's not worth it, but down deep, we know we need it. We know that no pain, no gain is true, and that goes for our spiritual lives as well as our physical bodies.

I told some men about this—men who are very successful in business, very good husbands and fathers. They said they could not imagine praying out loud with their families. It would embarrass them.

I said, "You mean you aren't afraid to take off your clothes in front of your wife, but you are afraid to pray out loud with her?"

That led to nervous laughter.

We don't want to be spiritually naked. So many people need us to be there, to cover them in prayer. And we need that, too.

11

Life Can Be So Tough

When I was a kid I had some arguments with my father. When I didn't know what else to say, I'd whine, "That's not fair."

"Who said life is fair?" he'd grunt.

My father was right. He also was expressing a biblical worldview, even though he didn't know it. He was just speaking from experience. Life is tough. Life is unfair. Life is one stupid thing after another. He was a man who grew up during the Depression and lived as if the "poor house" was real and we all could end up there. He was the first member of his family to graduate from high school, the first to grow up with English as his primary language. He served in the army during World War II. He worked for nearly thirty years at a food warehouse, rose from being a laborer to supervisor, and then was forced out of his job at the age of fifty-five when a new management team determined that he and other older employees were making too much money.

All that work, all those years, all of it added up to take a 50 percent pay cut and work the night shift, or take a hike.

None of it was fair.

I remember coming home from college early one afternoon in the middle of the week. I was commuting to school, trying to keep expenses down. My father seldom came home before 7 P.M. But he was there at his desk, bills spread out, saying nothing. Just staring. He wouldn't say what was wrong. Later, my mother explained it to me. He had quit rather than be humiliated by the company that had meant so much to him

for so long. He believed if you worked hard enough, kept
your mouth shut, and followed the rules, you'd end up okay.

He did all that but they still forced him out.

He worked several jobs after that, but none with nearly the
same pay or prestige that he once had at the warehouse. It
was a devastating blow to his self-esteem and to his vision of
how life should be lived. He never talked much about it. Kept
quiet, sucked it up, moved on. No time for whining. I don't
think he ever fully dealt with the grief and pain of what happened to him. He just stuffed it down and made it clear that
we weren't to discuss it.

I once heard someone say, "Life stinks, then you die." Many
of us have had the same feeling during trials and setbacks.

Jesus said in Matthew 6:33: "Do not worry about tomorrow, for tomorrow will worry about itself. Each day has trouble enough of its own."

Amen to that!

I was taught that people are generally good, that they at
least intend to do the right thing. This matched what I wanted
to think of myself, that I am a good, caring, unselfish guy,
even when I'm not acting like one.

"If that's the case," a friend once asked, "then how come
you have to teach a bunch of two-year-olds to share?"

At first I was confused by the question.

What does a two-year-old have to do with this debate about
people being selfish or unselfish? But I began to see the point.
If people are naturally decent and unselfish, why does it seem
one of the first words children learn is *mine?* How come they
are so easily jealous of and competitive with their siblings and
friends? Why will they tell blatant lies at such a young age?

Any parent can tell stories similar to the one about a tod-
dler covered with gooey chocolate. The stuff is all over him,
all over the floor, all over the walls, and he was the only one in
the room. You ask the child, "What happened here?"

He looks at you as if you're delusional, and says, "What?"

You say, "What do you mean, what? This mess. You're full of chocolate. Didn't I tell you not to touch that chocolate until Mommy came back?"

"You did?"

"I was looking right at you. I know you heard me," you say.

He hesitates for a moment, and then says, "I didn't do it."

"You didn't do it? Then who did?"

"I don't know."

You say, "You didn't make this mess?"

The child pauses, then blurts, "NO!"

"Then who did?"

He repeats, "I don't know."

While this ridiculous conversation is taking place, you're thinking, "How can this child of mine act like this? He's turning into a little liar. I can't believe it!"

Children don't come out of the womb as a next Mother Teresa, but as little tyrants who want what they want and want it now. They are willing to yell and cry and make everyone miserable until they get what they want.

Otherwise, why do we sometimes tell a pouting teen or angry adult to "quit acting like a two-year-old?"

That's not exactly a compliment. Obviously, some children are calmer and more teachable than others. But all of them must be taught to be polite and unselfish, to share and to play nice. Some learn those things faster than others, but very few come to those virtues naturally.

Maybe you disagree; you want to think the best of people. Maybe you're insulted by the idea that down deep, most of us fight the urge to act like spoiled two-year-olds. But think about what happens in most families, especially how easy it is to be resentful of how we are treated by our parents or siblings. Think about when we have to get to work and we're on a tight schedule, but a friend calls and wants to talk and talk, and yes, the friend is lonely and hurting, but it's the same old stuff over and over.

Or how about this? What percentage of our thoughts each day are about *us,* and what percentage of our thoughts each day are about *everyone else*? If we're honest with ourselves, we know the breakdown is not even close to fifty-fifty.

Whenever something happens, isn't it natural to ask, "How does this affect me?" Why is it so tempting to agree when someone says, "You have to look out for yourself because no one else really will?"

This is not meant to transform us into paranoids who believe everyone is a selfish clod out to get what he or she can. The world can be a very crazy place, and there are times when people really are out to get us, just as there are moments when we become obsessed with sticking it to someone else.

Let's make this personal. Why can I act like such a jerk?

This is true when I don't get my way and it seems someone else is getting a break that I deserve. I look at other writers' books and think, "That guy can't even put a decent sentence together and it's a best-seller. I'm writing these wonderful books, and no one reads them!"

Ever notice how we so easily make a case for ourselves being underpaid or underappreciated? We quickly think of someone making more money or receiving greater praise than we do, and we know they don't deserve it. But how many of us ever look around and think, "That poor woman over there, she works hard, never complains, does a great job, and doesn't make half as much as me?"

We find the slacker to make our case stronger, not the dedicated employee who continually outworks us. At least, I do.

Sometimes, I wish everyone would smarten up and just listen to me. For example, I've said, "Why can't we all just get along?"

Of course, the best way to do that is for everyone to do things my way.

Isn't that a little selfish?

The Bible tells us that people have been operating on their own agendas since the dawn of time. When Adam and Eve were in the garden of Eden, they had total peace and harmony with God. It was paradise. But they were tempted by the devil, disobeyed the only commandments given them by God. Then they were kicked out of this little bit of heaven on earth. In Genesis 3:1–24 there is an account of what is known as "the Fall of Man." The bottom line of the story is that we live in a world that's a mess.

There are times when I want heaven on earth, and I want it now. I want everyone to operate on my schedule. But that's just not going to happen.

It makes sense to want justice, peace, and fairness. All of those are admirable goals, and we should strive for them. By making some of these things a priority—helping the poor, pushing for peace, defending the rights of the oppressed—we do make the world a better place. But I still believe it's always going to be a mess, that life will always be tough.

There is a famous story about a child on a beach littered with thousands of starfish that had washed ashore. A man sees the child picking up the starfish one at a time and putting them back into the water. The man tells the child that it's impossible to save them. The child says it's worth it to save at least one. Sometimes, the child is each of us, helping one person through one crisis at a time. And sometimes, we are like the unsuspecting starfish because a tidal wave of sorts has blown us out of our comfort zone and tossed us onto the hot sand. We really were in the wrong place at the wrong time.

So don't be shocked when life turns ugly, when all our breaks seem to be fractures.

If you read the four New Testament gospels closely, you

will find people who wanted Jesus to heal them all, to overthrow the Roman government, and to deal with the cold hearts found in religious establishments. Jesus is like the child on the beach, saving soul after soul, healing body after body, and at the same time warning about more trouble to come.

Remember, Jesus didn't say, "Get in my Mercedes and ride with me." He said, "Take up your cross and follow me."

That's life today. It's tough. Sometimes, we build our own cross. Other times, the cross just drops on us. Either way, it's heavy and we all need God's help to carry it around.

12

Do You Have a Secret Fear?

Secret fears.

Most of us have them, even if we don't realize it.

The child of the alcoholic grows up not drinking a drop, still scared that one day she'll wake up and be a drunk like Mom. The man who was raised hearing that his grandfather, his father, and every other no-account male in his family went to jail is afraid he'll end up there, too.

There's the woman who watched her mom die of breast cancer. The man who saw his father drive the family into bankruptcy. Those of us who have Alzheimer's in the family, or perhaps a mental illness, start to wonder if we're losing it when we forget a name or forget where we left the keys.

Secret fears.

I wrote a story about Jack Greynolds, the famed Barberton High School basketball coach who died at the age of seventy-three. His death came eighteen years after he had a stroke, eighteen years where he was unable to speak, drive, read, or take care of some very basic personal needs. I listened to Jackie Greynolds talk about his dad before the funeral, and I kept thinking about my father. I thought about how my father had a stroke at seventy-three and was in even worse shape than Jack Greynolds. My father changed from a strong, self-assured man to someone who needed help getting dressed, paying bills, getting through daily life. My father dreaded being a burden to his family, and died believing that he had become just that.

Secret fears.

Not long after talking to Jackie Greynolds about his dad, I felt a tightness in the chest, a sense of anxiety that I couldn't explain. Then I realized that I had looked stroke in the eye once again, and I blinked. Down deep, I am afraid of having a stroke. I have read about stroke symptoms: numbness, tingling, blurred vision, strange headaches. I know about all these and more. I certainly don't think about a stroke every day or even every month. But once in a while, the fear is there.

My secret fear has nothing to do with keeping my weight down, exercising, and eating right. It's not about avoiding stress (as if any of us can do that!). It's not entirely rational.

But it's real.

I don't want to end up like my father, in a wheelchair, in diapers, unable to speak, not thinking clearly. I don't want people to feel sorry for me. I don't want to be so helpless. I don't want people to look at me and think, "Didn't he used to be Terry Pluto? Wasn't he a sportswriter or something? Now look at him, the poor guy."

I called out to God in prayer. I realized that I needed to tell someone about this fear. I needed someone to pray with me about it. I told my wife and a few friends, and we prayed together. There came a sense of peace, at least for now. The fear was no longer secret, and suddenly, it didn't seem so scary.

Secret fears.

A friend told me about attending a seminar with some prominent professional men and women. The speaker asked them to write their fears on a card, no names attached. What scared most of these successful people?

Being "found out." Not that they cheated to get their jobs, but that the rest of the world would discover that they aren't really talented. These professionals remembered days of feeling overmatched and underprepared, days when they were just thankful no one noticed they were shaking inside.

According to several surveys, one of people's biggest fears

is public speaking, because there's a real chance you'll make a fool of yourself in front of a crowd.

We have fears we won't meet expectations at work, at home, with friends. We have a fear that we won't make enough money; or maybe, that we'll make too much money and we won't know how to handle it wisely. I know athletes who have battled that problem. Who wants to be known as someone blessed with money they can't handle? That would be humiliating.

Secret fears.

I actually understand that feeling. I'm fifty. I've been a full-time sportswriter for twenty-eight years. I've been writing for money since I was eighteen. I've won a lot of awards, but when a few years pass and I don't win some of the bigger ones, I pretend it doesn't matter. I tell everyone, "Never worry about awards. They are completely subjective. Just be thankful when you do win, and don't sweat it when you don't."

Still, part of me wonders whether I'm losing my edge when contest winners are announced and I'm passed over. I've seen writers who are like ballplayers, still at it way past their prime, with no one to tell them that it's time to quit. Down deep, they know it's time. But they love what they do. I remember a veteran pitcher telling me, "Just when I really figured out this game, I was too old to play it."

The same can be said of most professions, or even life itself.

Secret fears.

Virtually every parent has secret fears. Am I doing the right thing for the kids? Am I doing the same stupid stuff my parents did? Am I equipped to handle this? Of course we don't do everything right all the time with kids. We catch ourselves repeating the same lame things our parents said to us—those things we promised that we'd never say to our kids. No one has all the answers for parenthood.

No one gets everything right in life.

Everyone is afraid of something.

In Philippians 4:5–7, Paul writes: "The Lord is near, do not be anxious about anything. In prayer and with thanksgiving, present your requests to God and the peace of God that transcends all understanding will guard your hearts and mind."

What are your secret fears? Begin to pray about them. Maybe you think you don't have any fears. Maybe that's true, but don't bet on it. Ask God to show your fears to you; do it through prayer. Sometimes a real fear is that we are afraid of something, that we're not as strong and mature as we think. Living in denial is fertilizing secret fears. Find out what scares you, and then remember that God already knows and wants to hear about it.

As Jesus said in Matthew 11:28–30, "Come to me, all you who are weary and burdened, and I will give you rest."

13

"Be like me."

It's a dumb question, but I still ask it: "Why can't he deal with a problem like I would? Why can't she see what needs to be done? It's obvious to me. If I were in his shoes or in her place, I'd . . ."

Of course, they are not me.

Most of us are wired to look at the world through our own eyes, and we wonder why others don't see the world the same way.

Ever say, "Can't we all just get along?" That often means, "Why can't we do things my way?" or "If we did things my way, it would be best for everyone." That's because a part of us believes that what's best for me is usually best for everyone else.

Or at least, I can talk myself into it because we believe one of the best sales pitches, which says, "Have it your way!"

Ours is a world that probably becomes more selfish every year. This is a major spiritual battle for me.

As a sports columnist, I'm paid to have opinions. A good column has a clear point, one that should be expressed forcefully. It's not about fairness, although my job is to be as fair as possible to all sides. But the bottom line in column writing is an opinion.

It's a job where I get to tell athletes what they should do, even though I was a lousy athlete when I actually tried to play their games—and I haven't gotten any better with age. I tell coaches what to do, even though I admit they know more about their sports than I do. I tell owners how to spend their money, even though I have no idea how to run a major business.

I've always been thankful that most of my columns deal with sports, which is not as important as foreign affairs, politics, and local news. It's one thing to be wrong about who the Indians should trade, it's another to be wrong about the Middle East. But it doesn't take long for me to fire off an opinion on almost anything, and I can do so with such conviction that I sometimes surprise myself.

This not always a godly way to live.

My wife is a very smart woman. When I'm talking to her, I need to remember that God gave me two ears and one mouth for a reason, which is to listen twice as much as I talk. It's easy for me to trample her with my opinions, to assume she thinks my way is the best way.

When I talk to my wife, I should follow the example of former New York Yankees shortstop Tony Kubek, who became a baseball broadcaster for several decades. Right next to his scorecard was a note with these words in capital letters: SHUT UP! Tony told me he kept the note because he tended to talk too much, to overexplain.

I plead guilty.

Proverbs 11:2 reads: "When pride comes, then comes disgrace, but with humility comes wisdom."

I remember hearing myself on tape asking questions of athletes and coaches. But my words really weren't questions; they were mini-speeches. The point of an interview is to get the subject to talk, not show the other person that I'm knowledgeable in his field. After all, they are the experts. There are times when I'm insecure talking to someone, so I tend to talk too much. I tend to tell him what I would do in his place. I tend to forget Proverbs 10:19: "When words are many, sin is not absent. But he who holds his tongue is wise."

I have improved in this area. Before I begin to ask someone a question, I tell myself, "Just ask a question, then *shut up*!"

It's amazing how much we can learn by not saying a word. And how little we learn when we talk too much.

I keep telling myself that instead of always thinking what I'd do if I happened to be in someone else's place, I should get to know the person, listen to him or her, and see if I have an idea of what's behind the person's thinking and actions.

Proverbs 10:31 reads: "The mouth of the righteous brings forth wisdom, but a perverse tongue will be cut out."

I know there have been times when I wished I had cut my tongue out because someone was trying to tell me something important, but I wouldn't be quiet long enough to listen.

"Everyone should be quick to listen, slow to speak and slow to become angry" is a powerful verse in James 1:19.

I have heard that the average adult waits about seventeen seconds before interrupting someone else in a one-on-one conversation. I would have heard more about this but I blurted out, "I bet that's right!"

I began to think about how I'll hear someone talk, and within a few seconds I'm formulating what I want to say. I stopped listening and just looked for a place to interject my thoughts. I've been learning to be quieter in professional interviewing situations, but too often I leave those qualities on the job. At home and with friends, they are even more important.

I also realize something else is happening. I think that by throwing out an opinion or giving some unsolicited advice, I can bring a fast end to the conversation. I really don't want to hear what the other person has to say; I just want it to be over. Or else, I'm sure I already know what they think, so I want to cut them short and get to my turn—after all, my voice is what matters most, right?

St. Francis once said, "Preach the gospel all the time. When necessary, use words."

Listening can be a true act of love. Listening is harder than talking, because it's time consuming and it's unselfish. It's admitting that other people are not like me, and they don't need to know what I think about everything. They often just need someone to treat them with enough respect to listen for a few moments.

Common sense is critical. Some people will just talk and talk and talk. But all of us know some people who are quiet, who need to be made to feel secure and important enough so they know we really do want to hear what they have to say. The greatest gift we can give these people is to remember that we do have two ears, and one mouth. That we can listen twice as much as we talk. That not all of our thoughts are worth expressing, and that others may have something they can teach us.

I'm going to promise God that each day I'll make time to listen to someone, or I'll call someone who could use a friendly ear.

Psalm 46:10 reads: "Be still, and know I am God."

We can be still and reflect God to others. We'll get to know them better and understand why they don't have to be like us.

14

Do You Keep a Sabbath?

I plead guilty.

I know that one day a week is supposed to be a day of rest, a day of worship, a day to get closer to God and family. I know all of that is a great idea. I know I should do it.

I don't.

I get to church nearly every Sunday, "home and road," as we say in the sports business, which means whether I'm at home or traveling. But I often leave church to hustle to a game. That's true at least twenty times a year, and there are only fifty-two Sundays.

I bet I write my newspaper column at least thirty Sundays each year. For sportswriters, the weekend usually is the heart of the workweek. It would be super if the work I did on Sundays was service to others. Sometimes that's the case when I speak in prison, at a church, or at the city mission. Or it can be when I take an elderly person to a service. But most often on Sundays I'm working at my job.

I know that one of the Ten Commandments is to keep holy the Lord's Day.

I know that Moses said in Genesis 16:31: "Tomorrow is to be a day of rest, a holy Sabbath."

I know that some faiths have lots of rules about what you can and can't do on the Sabbath.

I know that Jesus went to the synagogue regularly.

I know that I need a Sabbath rest. I know that I seldom take it.

I can give you all the excuses. We live in a 24/7 world where nearly every business is open every day. Some are open every day and night. Sunday "Blue Laws" and other restrictions on trade and activities have gone the way of the hula hoop and the black-and-white TV. There are times when most of us simply must work on the Sabbath to keep our jobs.

I'm not talking about the exceptions when we simply must work. I'm talking about how I regularly break the rule about resting on the Sabbath.

Guess when I'm writing this chapter? You got it—Sunday night!

Guess what I just read?

In Exodus 31:14–17, God tells Moses: "Observe the Sabbath because it is holy to you. Anyone who desecrates it must be put to death. Whoever does work on that day must be cut off from his people. For six days, work is to be done. But the seventh day is a Sabbath of rest, holy to the Lord. Whoever does any work on the Sabbath must be put to death."

Christians can say they live in the age of grace, the age of the New Testament church where rules are not too rigid. In Mark 2:24–25, Jesus is challenged by the religious elite because some of his disciples were hungry and they gathered corn as they walked through a field. In other instances, Jesus was criticized for healing people on the Sabbath.

Jesus responded, "The Sabbath was made for man, not man made for the Sabbath. So the Son of Man is Lord, even on the Sabbath."

His point was that God doesn't need anything from us. But we need to rest and worship at least one day a week. Even if you have absolutely zero faith, it's hard to argue with that.

Yet, I violate the rest and worship rule all the time.

My job is different from many others. I don't have to be at a certain place unless there's a game that I'm assigned to write about. I can make my own schedule. I must make sure that I complete my stories on time, and that I regularly produce for the paper.

I don't *have* to work nearly as many Sundays as I do. Yes,

on sixteen Sundays each year the Browns play. I may miss one game each season. The Browns are a big part of my job. I'll write stories on other Sundays simply because I have an idea and some free time.

But this is time when I should be resting, time when I should be talking to my wife, time when I should pray or read a spiritual book, time when I don't need to work.

Some religions have argued about what day constitutes the Sabbath. Some say Sunday, others insist it is Saturday. Or maybe it's part of both days, having to do with sunsets and sunrises.

The bottom line is still rest and worship.

As for God wanting people put to death for working on the Sabbath, it seems God is probably talking about how many people die from overwork. The older I get, the more I realize that God's basic commandments don't make my life harder, just better. That's true even when the commandments are challenging and restrictive.

For example, if I went through life never being jealous, never coveting other people's stuff or even their relationships, I'd be a happier, healthier person. I can't think of a single instance where a lie helped me in the long run. It's difficult to make a solid case for murder or adultery being useful activities.

Yet, keeping the Sabbath is on the list of commandments and I consistently ignore it. I know I need rest. I know it now at age fifty better than I did when I was forty.

The best idea I have come up with to fulfill this commandment is to pick another day and make it a day of rest.

So many people work on Sundays. So many people work overtime, work six days a week, work two jobs. We work and work and work.

Boston College professor Juliet Schor wrote a book called *The Overworked Americans*, about how we're working harder and longer now than we were in the 1950s, or even the '70s.

Her research showed that most people work ten to twenty more hours per week than in the days when most worked Monday through Friday or about forty hours a week. In terms of sheer hours, we are working more like we did during the Depression, although both economic and working conditions are better now than in the 1930s. It's primarily a result of a society that never rests, that expects certain businesses to be open every day, all the time.

So what should we do?

Most of us know some version of Matthew 11:28: "Come to me all you who are heavy burdened and I will give you rest."

That is Jesus speaking, and his words still have power. God wants us to take a Sabbath rest.

As Jesus said in Matthew 12:11–12: "If any of you has a sheep that falls into a pit on the Sabbath, will you not take hold of it and lift it out? How much more valuable is a man than a sheep? Therefore, it is lawful to do good on the Sabbath."

Jesus was dealing with some religious people who were upset because he healed people on the Sabbath. It's why we need doctors, police, firefighters, and other emergency personnel working weekends. But they and we can't work *every* day. Not without falling apart physically and mentally, and perhaps making poor decisions from fatigue.

That's why we need to take a Sabbath rest, even if it's in the middle of the week. For a while, I was reasonably dedicated to selecting a day when I would do no writing for work or for books. My Sabbath could be a Wednesday, when I spend mornings helping teach a jail bible class or conduct a service. Even I was surprised at how soon I simply abandoned this Sabbath goal. Within a few months, I was back to making calls, writing stories, doing something nearly every day of the week. I stopped marking my day of rest on my calendar. I didn't bother to mention it to my wife. I just said, "I take every day as it comes and find a Sabbath."

Lousy planning leads to lousy plans doomed to fail.

That was my approach to the Sabbath. I make time to go to church, which is a great idea. At my church, I always feel welcome and refreshed. The preaching is powerful, the prayers sincere, the atmosphere usually dominated by the spirit of God.

But I know that I still need to connect to God on my own, and to do it on God's time, not on my schedule.

If I want a Sabbath rest, then I need to plan it. I need to write it down, in ink. I need to stick with it, unless there is a real emergency. I need to believe that a relationship with God is as important as I say it is, that it matters at least as much as a business meeting. If I block out the time and clear my schedule for business, why can't I do the same for God?

FAITH
EVERY DAY

15

Can You Say No?

Ever notice how some people who sincerely love the Lord will sincerely make some promises and then just not deliver?

This happens all the time, especially in churches and temples. People want to be nice. They want to be godly. They want to do the right thing. Someone asks for a favor. They don't want to disappoint. They agree. They know down deep, their *yes* is not a *yes*.

At best, it's a *maybe*.

And that's wrong.

The Bible doesn't tell us to be a nice person who doesn't offend anyone. It calls us to be honest. I have dealt with this phenomenon myself in attempts to sell book ideas to some Christian publishers. As I've told my wife, "These people can't even reject you the right way!"

They talk about how they like some things in the book, and that some other things need work. They talk about wanting to be godly publishers, but how they also have business pressures. They talk about being a ministry, and they talk about wanting to sell books and make money. They talk and talk and talk.

I'm ready to scream, "*Just say it, you don't want my book! I'm a big boy, I can handle it.*"

It's the same in life.

You ask someone for a favor, and they seem to say they'll be there for you. But they don't show up. They don't call. Why can't they just say *no*?

"There's nothing wrong with telling someone that you'd

love to help him, but you just can't," said the Reverend Ronald Fowler of Arlington Church of God.

Don't pretend you might be able to fit it in. Don't hint that you'll take care of it later. Don't worry about what someone may think if you turn him or her down. Be more concerned about how they will feel if you let them down.

I sound harsh about this, but I really believe it's a character flaw. Some people want to avoid conflict regardless of the circumstances, so they say anything just to get through a situation. When you confront these types about their unfulfilled promises to help, they look at you strangely, as if *you* did something wrong. It's almost as if they're saying, "What's your problem? I meant to come when I said I would. Besides, you're supposed to be a person of faith, a forgiving person. You know how it is when you get busy."

What we *know* is that the person made a promise but didn't deliver. That made it harder for everyone else who did keep their word.

When Jesus gave his famous Sermon on the Mount talk in Matthew 5:1–12, one of the messages was "Simply let your Yes be Yes, and your No be No. Anything beyond this comes from the evil one."

That's why I annoy some people when they ask me, "Can you do me a favor?"

I always say, "It depends."

They usually are surprised that I didn't just agree. They're thinking, "I thought Pluto was supposed to be a decent guy."

I tell them, "You may want my wallet. You may want to borrow my car. You may want me to do something that I can't do. I'm not going to say I'll help until I know what you want."

They laugh.

I don't.

There have been times in my life when I have let others down because I wanted to be a "nice guy." I was worried more about my reputation than their needs.

"A lot of people sincerely mean well," said Fowler. "But they get themselves way overextended. The urge to please is natural. But the failure to follow up is destructive."

Fowler told the story of how Jesus cursed a fig tree and it died (Mark 11:12–14). "When a fig tree had leaves it was supposed to have fruit," he said. "But in this case, the tree had leaves. It looked good. But it produced nothing."

God is not pleased with people who sound good but whose promises are empty.

"There is only so much anyone can do," said the Reverend Knute Larson of the Chapel. "Jesus must have told people 'no' sometimes. There were times when he went to get away from everyone."

We know we can't do it all, so why try to fool ourselves or anyone else? We want to be nice; we want to be liked. We are afraid to be honest.

"More important than being nice is having integrity," said Fowler. As Proverbs 13:6 reads: "Righteousness guards those with integrity."

Fowler explained that something else happens when you fail to follow up on your word: people often feel guilty. "Then they avoid the person they promised to help, and that leads to even more problems than just saying 'no' in the first place."

Yet another problem. The person who didn't keep his word is embarrassed, so he acts as if he doesn't see you. Or when you do make contact, he acts like nothing happened; he pretends nothing is wrong.

Larson mentioned that Jesus talks about "yes" and "no" right after saying we should not have to take any oaths.

"That's because every word from our mouth should be as good as an oath," Larson said. "I grew up in a church setting where they said there should be no need to take an oath in court. You should be truthful at all times."

That means sometimes saying no even if people take it personally or try to pressure us.

"Someone will ask me to speak and I'll turn them down because I'm already scheduled to be somewhere else," Larson said. "The person will ask me to pray about it."

In most cases, there is nothing to pray about. Your schedule is already overstuffed. Or you're tired. Or you know this is not a good idea for you. It's obvious that it won't work.

Yet, some people will try to play the guilt card when we decline. For example, I've had people say, "And I thought you were a Christian."

I may be, but I'm not a miracle worker. I can't be in two places at once. None of us can be everything to everyone. As Chuck Colson, the former Watergate figure turned prison minister, said: *Every need is not a call.*

I really like that message: *Every need is not a call.*

There are so many good causes, so many things we can do that are worthwhile. But we can't do them all. In many cases, we're not supposed to do them. Our goal should not be to have a job, raise a family, be a spouse, and spend five nights a week on church or ministry activities. Not unless we plan to burn out our souls and burn bridges with those who were counting on us.

Every need is not a call.

There are times in the Bible when people want Jesus to preach, to heal, to be in the crowd, but he leaves them to rest and pray in the mountains. All of those people's needs were good, but Jesus knew he couldn't meet every call.

That applies to all of us. I tell myself it's easier to change a "no" to a "yes" than a "yes" to a "not." It's better to underpromise and overproduce, because that way you don't disappoint.

That way your "yes" and your "no" really do mean something.

16

Consider a Jerk Fast

Fasting, now there's a scary word.

For me, it was about not eating meat on certain days, or the thought of some gaunt monk on a mountain starving himself as tries to get closer to God. I knew that some people didn't eat for days.

I had no interest in any of it.

But I kept reading about people in biblical times fasting. I've met people who would skip a meal before they had to give a speech. Even if it didn't get them closer to God, it probably prevented a nervous stomachache. That kind of fasting may have been more practical than spiritual.

I go through periods when I want my Everyday Faith to grow, and I've tried fasting. I was interested in trying to make a special season of Lent—those forty days between Ash Wednesday and Easter. I wanted to give up something for God. I also wanted to see if I could really do it and if it meant anything in my prayer life.

Besides, I had been drinking too much diet soda and I knew I had to cut back. The first two weeks of my soda fast felt like forty years. It may not sound like a big deal unless you happen to be a Diet Pepsi addict like me. That's a nice way of saying I'm a caffeine addict.

I made it Pepsi-free for forty days. That meant no Pepsi of any kind, not even Pepsi Free.

I might have cheated if you consider that I started drinking diet ice tea. My guess is that there was a jolt of caffeine in there. But I was proud to complete forty days without any sort of diet cola, and it's been decades since I was able to go without it for that long.

Does this make me any more spiritual? Obviously not.

Is it a good idea?

Everyone from the Old Testament prophets to Jesus prayed and fasted. Sometimes, they didn't eat anything. Other times, theirs were specialized fasts, not eating certain foods.

The idea of fasting for Lent, or for anything else, is to grow closer to God. It should be something that makes us more godly. Fasting is breaking our routine and doing something that honors God.

That's why fasting doesn't have to be about food, although some of us would have a better quality of life for forty days without Twinkies, barbecue potato chips, or double Whoppers.

Fasting is really about a D-word that I dread. (No, not donating, although giving some extra money or time each week is a great way to celebrate Lent.) The D-word is Discipline.

I really like Diet Pepsi. No, it's more than that. I'm like an alcoholic whose mouth waters every time he sees a blinking beer sign or hears a beer commercial on TV.

We have become like Pavlov's dogs when it comes to some of this stuff. Resisting the cola ads during my fast became a battle, and I began to enjoy it. Okay, not *enjoy* it, but appreciate that my life could use a little discipline and here was a chance to show it.

I know some people shouldn't fast for medical and other physical reasons. Others already have eating disorders, and the last thing they need is fasting. But there are other types of fasts that make sense.

I've suggested a "man fast" or a "woman fast." Quit dating or looking for dates for two months. We can get so hungry for a relationship, we'll settle for almost anything. We become like a desperate shopper at midnight on Christmas Eve; rational thinking has been replaced by an obsession not to go home empty.

Buy an electric shoehorn for your uncle. If nothing else, it's unique, right?

Some people consistently date "unique" people whom their friends would call something else.

They'd say, "She's just weird," or "He's pretty creepy." Or, "Have you checked how many times this person already has been married, and whether this person has been in jail lately?"

This is easy for me to say because I've been married for twenty-eight years and my wife is God's greatest gift to me, after my life of faith. Whenever I want a date, I have one. And it's with the person who'd always be my first choice anyway. I do remember a time in the distant past when I wish someone had told me, "Just stop hunting for romance and try to find a deep relationship with God."

I may not have listened to that advice, but I still needed to hear it.

Many people need to heal from all the broken hearts and pointless nights trying to impress someone they don't respect.

Maybe your relationships are fine, but maybe money is your problem. How about a credit card fast? Can you go six weeks without the plastic? Or maybe limit credit purchases to one every ten days. Bet you'd be surprised what you can live without.

Others may be hooked on TV. Do we need to watch all those soap operas, including the trashy ones at night that bill themselves as dramas? Or the worm-eating reality shows? Or how about sports? Do we need to watch *every* game? Why not try a TV fast by saying, "I'll watch just one trash show each week." Or "I'll watch only the Cavaliers, and skip the rest." You could use the rest of the time to talk to your spouse and kids.

How about setting aside a little time each day to pray with your spouse, with a parent, a friend, the children? Or try to get back into church a little more?

What about an e-mail fast every week for twenty-four hours—no computer. I know I waste so much time reading and answering e-mail that has no impact on my life. Each year I vacation in Wyoming for two weeks where there's no computer, no TV. After a few days, I don't even miss it. But when I'm home . . .

A twenty-four-hour e-mail fast once a week is next for me now that Lent is over and I'm back to Diet Pepsi, okay, a few Diet Pepsis.

We do have an enemy who tempts us. That's why we have sudden cravings to watch stupid TV shows while eating a gallon of Moose Tracks ice cream. It's why we head to the mall with no mission other than "I gotta buy something to make me feel better." It's why I sometimes want a Diet Pepsi first thing in the morning.

That temptation means many of us will mess up our best promises to God.

Don't give up. Psalm 145:14 reads: "The Lord upholds all who fall and lifts up all who are bowed down."

I like that because I fall a lot. I also keep getting back up after being discouraged and beating myself up. A little guilt or pity party never hurt anyone.

Another verse I like is Psalm 37:24: "Though he stumbles, he will not fall. The Lord upholds him with his hand." It tells us, don't listen to that voice that says, "You can't ever stick to anything."

When I fast, sometimes I follow through, sometimes I don't. But I've stopped kicking myself when I blow it.

Over the years, I have taken to skipping a nightly meal when I have something important that evening or the next morning. I don't claim any special power from this kind of fast. I'm not telling anyone to do the same thing. I do think it takes some practice, but it also produces some clarity of thought. Obviously, if there are medical reasons, then eat! I've heard idiotic stories of people fasting and skipping their medicine, believing God will heal them. Hey, God made medicine too, and as one pastor said, "It's a sin not to use it!"

That's why I like a behavior fast rather than a food fast. It can make a bigger impact on our lives.

In Matthew 6:16, Jesus said, "When you fast, don't look somber as the hypocrites do, for they disfigure their faces to show they are fasting." I always love it when Jesus takes off on the "holier than thou" crowd.

Fasting is optional, but don't be a jerk about it.

In fact, that may be the basis of my new jerk fast! I'm going to quit hanging out with jerks and quit acting like a jerk. Now that will take some work.

17

Why Do We Like to Believe Gossip?

At least a few times each week, someone wants to tell me a story about a well-known player or a coach. It's usually not a nice story. It usually won't make the newspaper, because no one can prove it. Usually, it's a little hard to believe.

But I listen . . . and I usually believe it.

I should know better. I've been the victim of gossip; we all have. A few years ago, there was a story about me having dinner with a woman in Tennessee. It was not my wife of twenty-eight years. This woman and I supposedly were not acting as if we were checking scouting reports for the upcoming NFL draft. Let's just say the meeting was supposedly far more personal than professional.

I was not in Tennessee at the time, as I told a few people who mentioned the story to me. I was grateful that some asked about it. Usually, we just talk about others, seldom going to the source to check out gossip. When I denied the rumors about me and explained that I had been in Tennessee but not at that time, the people who talked to me seemed relieved. They said they didn't believe what they had heard; they just wanted me to know. They couldn't even remember where they'd heard the story. You know how it goes, right?

I'm sure some people believed it, people who should know better.

That's because there is a part of us that wants gossip to be fact. Maybe that's not true of everyone, but I know I fight that urge. I hear stories and I just know they can't be true. I know the subject of the story rather well. But then I think of times when I have heard something about another person—something outrageous and out of character that turned out to be true.

Why is it that we remember the stories that turn out to be true, but forget the ones that can never be proved or are just plain wrong?

When I hear things part of me says, "Well, I really don't know most people very well." That's a way of saying that the gossip may be true. We live in a crazy world and anything is possible.

A friend told me the story of a partner in his firm whom he had known for years. Suddenly, the partner vanished. His wife was dead. He killed her and left the country. He had never had any problems with the law; there was never any indication the marriage was in trouble. But the wife was dead, the guy gone, his friends stunned.

It seems anyone can steal. Anyone can have an affair. Anyone can act like a jerk, as long as that *anyone* is not me!

A rabbi told me the story of a famous Jewish rabbi many centuries ago who was the victim of gossip. The man who started the story confessed to the rabbi. He had been upset about something the rabbi had said, and he spread a vile rumor.

The rabbi said, "It is good that you have apologized."

The man said, "I'll go to the people who heard the story from me and tell them it's not true."

The rabbi said, "I have a request."

The man said, "Anything, just ask."

The rabbi said, "Take a pillow to town. When you get to Main Street, wait for a great wind. When it blows, cut the pillow open and shake out all the feathers."

The man said that sounded strange, but he'd do it.

The rabbi said, "Then I want you to go all over town and gather up every single feather from that pillow."

"I'll never get back all the feathers," the man said.

The rabbi said, "That's how it is with gossip."

Isn't that the truth? Once the story is out, it's like the wind. Who knows where it will go?

Another version of that story is in the terrific book *The Committed Life* by Rebbetzin Esther Jungreis. In this account, the rabbi tells the man to put a feather in the front of every house where he spread gossip, then return to the rabbi. When the man returns, the rabbi says, "Now, go back and gather up the feathers."

The man says, "I'll never get them all." And we get the point.

In her book, Jungreis wrote that her rabbi husband often said, "There are two ways for a person to become taller. The first is by climbing a ladder; the second is by pushing others down. It takes less effort to push others down than to raise yourself up."

Proverbs 25:18 reads: "Like a club or a sword or a sharp arrow is the man who gives false testimony about his neighbor."

In some ways, gossip is worse than a physical attack.

If you're physically assaulted, you're usually viewed as a victim. People side with you. Your attacker may be arrested.

But if you're the target of gossip, you show no physical signs of harm. It's just your reputation that takes a beating. Rarely is anyone ever held responsible.

Proverbs 10:11 reads: "The mouth of the righteous is a fountain of life, but violence overwhelms the mouth of the wicked."

Maybe gossip is not a problem for you, but it is for most people. Otherwise, why would so many celebrity gossip shows pollute TV? Why do so many supermarket tabloids sell millions of copies? And why do I find myself staring at the covers of those tabloids while I'm in line at the grocery store?

And why do I want to pick them up and read about the famous people who trashed their lives?

Proverbs 10:18: reads: "Whoever spreads slander is a fool."

But sometimes, he can be a rich fool, especially in my business.

I struggle with gossip because information fuels the media. One of the best ways to get information from a source is to trade information. No one calls it a trade, of course, but you tell someone something you've heard, and he or she tells you something. Before you know it, the conversation sinks into something like "Then this idiot told the coach to . . . "

In church circles, one of the ways to spread gossip is through a prayer request. Someone will say, "We need to pray for Mary." Another will ask why. The first person says, "Because I hear that her husband is having an affair."

It's all in the name of prayer, right? Why not just put an advertisement in the church bulletin? We can be so phony.

In James 3:3–5, the author writes: "The tongue is a small part of the body, but it makes great boasts. Consider what a great forest is set on fire by a small spark. The tongue also is a fire."

Just as feathers are carried away by the wind, so it is easy for anyone to be burned by gossip. Gossip brings out the worst in us, especially when we try to act like it's really not gossip. Even if it's true that Mary's husband is having an affair, do we need to tell everyone about it? Can't we just keep it to ourselves and pray? Spreading this news won't help their marriage, and might make it worse.

At times, I just pray, "God, help me to get through today without gossip."

I have learned to walk away from some conversations. When a person wants to tell me something that I know is headed straight into the pit of gossip, I'll try to say, "I know that Joe has problems. I really don't need to hear any more. The poor guy is a mess." Then I try to change the subject.

I'm not always successful. And I'm too often tempted to ask about what Joe did now, because gossip is fun to hear. It does raise us up in a perverse way by shoving others down.

Before I pass on information, I try to ask myself, "Does anyone really need to hear this? Is there a way to deal with this subject without passing on gossip?"

Most of the time, there *are* better, godlier, ways to communicate. But those require work. And the first part of that effort is remembering how we feel when we are the targets of gossip.

18

Do You Visit the Sick?

When my father had his stroke, we found out who his real friends were.

He had lost the ability to speak, the ability to walk, the ability to use his right arm and leg. He was not easy to be around because he could say only one word, "man." It made it impossible to hold any sort of conversation with him, especially for those not used to his speech and the frustration he'd show when he couldn't communicate. His face would turn red; he'd just start saying, "Man, man, man" louder and faster while pointing at something. You'd guess at what he wanted, and usually you'd be wrong. He would just shake his head "no," almost violently.

The people he bowled with may have come by once, but that was it. Others he knew from bingo just realized that he no longer showed up for the games, and word was he'd had a major stroke. They forgot about it. This is not to put down my father's friends; it's just true that most people don't want to visit the sick, especially those who are disabled and perhaps near death.

I'm not much different. I had to learn to get over my aversion to hospitals when I was helping to care for my father. I had no choice. He lived for nearly five years after the stroke, and eighteen months of that time was spent in medical and rehabilitation centers.

I thought about visiting sick people when I received an e-mail from the son of a former co-worker. He said his father was in a hospital, extremely ill with cancer. He said his father always liked me. I had not seen his dad in at least eight years. He said his dad could use some visitors, but not to expect much. His dad was in very bad shape.

I didn't want to go. But then I thought of my father, and how so few people came to see him. He had a friend named Louise, who'd drop by a few times each week to play cards. I still thank God for Louise, who wasn't bothered by my dad's speech. She just talked and talked. He could still play cards. She was a hairdresser and she would cut Dad's hair; did that every few weeks, and it became a big deal.

I thought of Louise, too, when I read the e-mail. So I went to see the former co-worker friend.

The moment I walked into the room, I knew he was dying. He was a little older than I am, but he looked almost like a child. He was in the hospital bed, pulling the covers close to his neck, shivering, eyes wide and frightened. I hadn't seen him for years when I heard he was ill. In this case, it was cancer. But I've had a few similar instances with people in the last inning of life. It's not pretty. My former co-worker was on heavy medication. He tried to talk, but the words wouldn't come.

I wondered, "Does he even know who I am?" He seemed aware that someone was in the room. I told him my name. He stared at me. I reached out and took his hand. He seemed pleased someone wanted to touch him. He hung on tight. That's when I realized why I was there: to touch this guy.

"Are you scared?" I asked.

He nodded.

He kept clearing his throat, trying to speak. It sounded like a car that wouldn't start, just growling, growling, growling. He had some fruit juice on the tray next his bed. I held it as he drank from the straw.

"Better," he said. It was the first time I understood a word.

"Two days," he said. "If I get home in two days . . . "

I nodded and sat there wondering what I should say. Does he hear me? What exactly is he hearing? I know that patients in his situation often drift in and out. Drugs will do that, one drug after another, each trying to combat different side effects, sometimes creating more suffering.

My friend was stuck on the two days. I asked him when he had gone into the hospital, and he said "Friday." Every few words were clear; the rest lost in the battle with the medication, the cancer, the frustration, the agony. I started to tell him about people we knew and experiences we shared.

For the first time, he smiled.

"Terry," he said. "It's bad." Then he closed his eyes. I wasn't sure if he went to sleep, or if it was just the pain. I sat there for a while. He had taken both of his hands and pulled the bed covers up under his chin. He sometimes rubbed his neck.

A nurse arrived.

"Onion soup," he said.

The nurse said, "We only have chicken and beef broth."

He nodded and closed his eyes. He never did decide on a soup flavor, and she said she'd return later. During this time, I had no idea what to do or what to say. I flashed back to the final months of my father's life, when he was dying from the stroke and heart failure. He couldn't do much besides sort of watch TV. But he wanted me there. I learned to sit next to him silently, to read a book, to occasionally reach out and take his hand.

I felt helpless and useless at those times. Still I knew visiting my friend was the right thing to do. I had given comfort to someone who needed it, someone who just wanted another person in the room. It's not very often that I feel God smiling on me, but I did that day.

Hospital visits don't always go this well, and, believe me, even that one was a struggle because the man couldn't communicate much. But they can be worse. Several months after the visit with my former co-worker, another e-mail came in. It was about someone in the hospice unit of an assisted living center. I barely knew the man, and I wrote back that I didn't think I had seen the guy in twelve years; we really weren't close once upon a time. Another e-mail came back, reminding me of a column that I had written urging people to visit the sick.

The challenge was obvious: Would I walk the talk? I put it off for a few weeks, and then finally made the visit. When I saw the man; his wife was there. She was outraged about the care they were receiving at the institution, which seemed to be a very nice place. Her husband had been ill that morning and no one seemed to care. A piece of furniture in the room was broken. Why wouldn't anyone listen to her?

I was thinking, "I barely know this guy, I don't know his wife at all, and I didn't even want to do this."

I explained to the woman why I was there, about the e-mail telling me that her husband would appreciate a visit. He was hooked up to an oxygen machine. I couldn't tell if he knew who I was; he just sort of smiled. She continued to complain, and I realized that the anger was directed more at life, or at the fact that her husband was dying. Maybe her anger was with God *because* her husband was dying. I was just another annoyance.

What I should have said was "I can see that you're really upset, I feel bad for you." But I didn't. I could have softened her spirit and given her a little comfort just by listening until she ran out of complaints.

But I didn't.

I just needed to show some love. I could have offered to pray for her and her husband.

But I didn't.

I took the attitude: "Hey, no problem, you want to be alone, go ahead." I was like some of my father's first visitors after his stroke. Being there was difficult, and I didn't want to deal with it.

I told her that I'd leave, and that I'd inform people that she needed some attention.

She seemed surprised and a little upset that I was leaving so soon. I had been there no more than fifteen minutes. I didn't care; I wanted out. I almost ran out of the room. When I left, I felt relieved but sad. The woman was hurting more than her husband, and I could have done more to help her.

When people are scared and frustrated, they can get angry. I suddenly realized that people who are close to the sick need visitors and patience, too. I should have remembered that from my experience with my father, but it's something that I forgot on that day.

I did talk to the staff about the situation in the man's room. They nodded and promised to check. I walked out knowing that I had visited the sick, but may as well have stayed home. I was there physically, but my heart was hard and elsewhere.

I only tell this story because people sometimes glamorize these visits, and they can be a challenge. I have friends who go room to room at a local hospital every Saturday. They are part of their church's hospital visitation team. They have prayed with patients moments before they died. They've prayed with families. They've watched ballgames on TV with sick people and read the Bible to others. They just go with the flow. A few times they've been told to take a hike because if there is a God, he's cruel to allow such pain and suffering.

But most of the sick are thrilled to see visitors. I remember visiting former *Akron Beacon Journal* columnist Fran Murphey when she was in hospice. I went a few times. She was so weak, she could barely speak. But she held my hand. She smiled. She whispered my name. She never really complained. She lifted me up, even if she usually fell asleep within fifteen minutes.

I know people who say they don't go to hospitals because it gives them the creeps. So what? One day, most of us will end up in places like that, waiting to die, not wanting to be alone. Most of us know visiting the sick is the right thing to do. The Bible tells us so in Matthew 25:34 when God says, "When I was sick or in prison, you visited me."

Being with my father at the end of his life taught me not to worry about what I'm supposed to do if someone is sick. I should just go and let God be my guide. If I have a lousy visit that doesn't mean I should stop visiting others. I shouldn't be afraid to pray with people; just take their hands and pray, out loud. It doesn't have to be long. It doesn't have to be poetry. It does need to come from the heart.

That's what I did with my old friend dying of cancer. It's what I did with Fran Murphey. It's what I hope I do with most of the people I see who are sick.

What do they hear or think about it? I have no idea. I just know that when I took my friend's hand, he clung to it. His lips seemed to move. We both felt a connection, and God was there.

19

Leave a Tip, Leave a Message

What does your tip say about your faith?

People should know that most waiters and waitresses are paid far below minimum wage. They depend on tips for their main income. Many are single parents. Others are working second jobs or trying to make enough money to pay for college. Very few of the people who bring you food and coffee are wealthy. Some are the definition of the working poor.

"That's one of the reasons we should treat these people with respect and be generous with tips," said the Reverend Knute Larson, pastor of the Chapel in Akron.

But waitresses will tell you that some of their worst tippers are people who come in to restaurants from churches or church services.

Here's an e-mail I got:

"Sundays tend to be an all-day affair of 10 percent tips, especially from families on their way home from church. More disturbing than the low tips was the treatment we received from people having just spent their mornings celebrating their religion. It's not uncommon for us to be treated like servants and ordered around without the smallest shred of manners or civility. Didn't these people just spend a few hours being taught to love their neighbors? Or don't we count?"

Another waitress wrote: "Sundays have become the one day most of us fear working."

Bad tips, worse manners.

A third waitress wrote, "Besides the poor tipping, even worse was the attitude of some 'Christian' patrons. One gentleman was always demanding and just plain cranky. One server finally said, 'Didn't you just come from church?' His wife laughed, but after that, he usually treated the servers with more respect. As a Christian, I am embarrassed by the actions of some of my own brothers and sisters in Christ."

These represent just a little of the feedback that came in when I first wrote a column for the newspaper about the subject of tipping and about how so many restaurant workers wished they could skip Sundays.

Barbara Ehrenreich gave her own "Amen" to the food servers' chorus in her book *Nickel and Dimed*. She worked at several low-paying jobs and then reported on the experience.

When she worked at a low-end restaurant in Florida, she wrote: "The worst, for some reason, are the Visible Christians—like the 10-person table, all jolly and sanctified after Sunday night service, who run me mercilessly and then leave $1 on a $92 bill. Or the guy with the crucifixion T-shirt who complains his baked potato is too hard, his iced tea too icy (I cheerfully fix both) and leaves no tip at all."

I know people will become defensive about this, but it's a story I hear over and over. Bill Hybells is the pastor of the well-known Willow Creek Church in the Chicago area. He gave a sermon and mentioned that the waitresses who work near his church—some even attend his church—told him that too many people from the church were cheap tippers and demanding, rude customers.

"I've heard that from my own daughter when she was a waitress," Larson said. "That really hurt me."

Granted, we're talking generalities. People who walk out of church and into a restaurant still in their Sunday best are perhaps watched more closely and judged more harshly.

"My guess is Christians usually tip pretty well, but when they don't, people notice," said Bishop Joey Johnson of the House of the Lord. "It's the old saying about how some of us are the only Bibles others will read. Let's face it; all of us are sinners. Not everyone is at the same spiritual level."

And some of us are just cheap and grumpy.

Larson said he's heard stories of waitresses finding a one-dollar tip in a little faith brochure. Or sometimes, food servers find no money at all, just the religious material.

Another waitress wrote: "Sometimes I've received a [religious] tract from the same people who know me fairly well. No one thought to ask if I was already a Christian. Some tracts are tasteless. My least favorite looks like a $100 bill. You open it up and it reads, 'Disappointed? You won't be if you have Jesus in your life.' Listen, I love Jesus, but must admit to being disappointed when I opened that and found only a dollar or two inside instead of $100. Wouldn't most of us be? This doesn't send a good message to those who work on Sundays so good people have a place to eat after church services."

Bible study groups meet at certain restaurants. These people generally stay at their tables for ninety minutes, not eating much. But they drink a lot of coffee and require more than the usual service.

"I tell our groups that they are renting the booth," Larson said. "You should tip at least 20 percent or more for something like that."

The general rule for tipping is 15 percent. Both Larson and Johnson said they usually tip at least 25 percent, often much more if the service is excellent. Obviously, there are times when the service is awful, the waiter or waitress moody, the food burned. There's no reason to reward that with a big tip.

When I made that point, I received an e-mail from someone who claimed to be Buddhist. This person said he believed Jesus would tip even higher for lousy service, giving to those who deserve it least. While Jesus didn't say much about tipping in the Bible, he did show mercy for those who honestly asked for mercy. He had very little patience with those who didn't seem to work hard or care about others. A basic 10 to 15 percent tip is all a lazy or angry server deserves.

Usually, food servers do a decent job in a very demanding

profession where they are on their feet hours at a time either cooking food or delivering it. Some people find it easier to open their wallets to the poor around the world than to the person who waits on them at the diner down the street.

"Christians are not all angels and saints," Johnson said. "Some may be saved in the eyes of God, but still be very damaged people. But you are a witness at work, at home, and when you go out to eat. You should be generous because God has been generous to you." Yes, but we forget to encourage and open our wallets to those who serve us.

I've heard from people who say they just hate tipping. They believe restaurants should pay their help better. Then tipping wouldn't be necessary. These people say that by tipping, we allow employers to get away with cheating the help.

Even if it's possible for employers to raise wages, the food service system is what it is. Not leaving a tip as a sign of protest hurts the server, who needs help the most. We can't control how restaurants pay their staff, but we have complete authority over how we tip.

Jesus said, "Do unto others as you'd have them do unto you."

Don't be stingy, leave that extra dollar or two.

Larson said there have been times when he has sneaked back to a table to add a few bucks to what he considered a cheap tip that someone in his party had left behind.

As for those who just refuse to leave a 15 percent tip? "If they are going to do that, then they should hide their Bibles when the waitress comes," Larson said. "A few people can give all of us a very bad name, and those waiting on us deserve better."

So what should we do? Tip as if your best friend is waiting on you. Or as Jesus said, "Do unto others . . . "

You know the rest.

20

Be Stingy with Loans

I never make a loan to a friend or a relative.

Perhaps you've never been in a situation where a friend or family member comes to you in desperate need. But just wait; that day is coming. Someone will need cash for school or to pay a pressing debt. He or she may want you to cosign a loan for a car or a house.

"Don't worry," he'll say. "You know I'm good for it. I'll repay. In fact, I'll pay you first. You can take my word."

Maybe you can. But have you ever been stiffed by someone close to you? Your relationship will never be the same, even if the financial situation eventually works out. Money divides far more families than it unites.

Still don't think so?

Just wait until a parent dies, and the siblings begin competing for parts of the estate. Watch the resentment bubble up, the venom spew from otherwise sane and kind people. Older siblings may think they are owed a special favor because they took care of younger kids. Younger siblings may believe it's time for them to cash in because the older children got special treatment simply because of age.

Families are flush with brothers and sisters who think they got a raw deal from their relatives. When money is on the line, relatives suddenly growl, bare their teeth, and get ready to rip each other apart.

Some people like to say that money is the root of all evil. That's pretty close to what Paul wrote in 1 Timothy 6:9–10: "People who want to be rich fall into temptation and a trap and into many foolish and harmful desires that plunge men into ruin and destruction. For the love of money is a root of all kinds of evil. Some people, eager for money, have wandered far from the faith and pierced themselves with many griefs."

So much truth in so few words.

I have lent money to people I knew, and I didn't like what happened to the relationship. Money can bring out the worst in us because it immediately sets up a power struggle. The one with the ready cash has some sort of control over the borrower, or at least he thinks he should.

And the person borrowing money may think, "Hey, I can stall him for a while; he's my friend."

Or, "She's my sister."

Or, "They're my parents, and they should support me."

Then the person who lent the money is thinking, "We're related by blood and this guy is treating me worse than he would treat a credit card company. At least he sends them a few bucks each month to keep them off his back."

The Bible tells us to be generous, as in Psalm 37:26: "They always lend freely, their children will be blessed."

But what if you lent a sizable amount of money to an adult child, as one parent I know did. It was supposed to be for a family business, but the business failed. The daughter filed for bankruptcy, and the parents never did get anything back. Their daughter claimed she worked hard to make the business successful. She said her parents should view their loan to her like any other business investment, and not take it personally.

When it comes to money between family and friends, how can it not be personal? Knowing the lender personally was the basis for the entire transaction. Most of the time in family situations, people lending money do it as an act of faith in the borrower. They are investing in the person.

In the former situation when the daughter's business collapsed, her parents were stunned. One of them told me, "If nothing else, I thought she'd pay us back first."

That's why so many family businesses have become family messes.

Proverbs 22:7 reads: "The rich rule over the poor, the borrower is servant to the lender."

The daughter didn't have to repay her parents. She declared bankruptcy, and put them on the same list with other creditors. None got paid. Legally, she got out of debt to them. But what about their relationship? It's one thing to declare bankruptcy because of credit cards. (So you never talk to Visa again? That may be a good thing.) But never talking to your parents again? Or feeling uneasy every time you do because of a business deal gone bad?

Proverbs 22:26 says: "Do not be a man who strikes hands in pledge or puts up security for debts. If you lack the means to pay, your very bed will be snatched from under you."

I know of a man who cosigned a loan for his son, who failed to make payments. The loan company came after the father, and he had to settle the loan by cashing accounts he had saved for his retirement. The father's credit rating also took a hit because he no longer was considered a preferred customer.

So what to do?

Here's an idea, but it's not in one of the Ten Commandments. It's not something set in stone or ethically clear. I've adopted what Jesus said in Luke 6:34: "If you lend to those from whom you expect payment, where is that a credit to you? Even sinners lend to sinners expecting to be repaid."

So when a friend or relative is in need, I don't lend them money. I either *give* it to them, or I turn them down.

A gift seems to work best for me because it takes the pressure off. I don't expect to be repaid. When I give someone money, I tell her that she doesn't have to return a cent. I don't worry about her repaying me, and she doesn't have to worry about paying. I insist that it won't change our relationship, and I pray that it doesn't. I say, "I'm sure you'd do the same for me if the situation were reversed."

When I was in the midst of taking care of my father after his stroke, his health-care bills mounted. My father-in-law asked if there was anything he could do to help. I told him I needed about ten thousand dollars, and I needed it soon. I was preparing to apply for a loan on my home. I told my father-in-law about the bills. He produced the ten thousand dollars. We worked out a payment plan, and his was the first check I wrote each month. I managed to pay him off early because some extra money came in from book royalties.

I did this before I developed my own rule about keeping personal relationships separate from business dealings. But I took the money, and my father in-law helped me in a rough spot. I also know that he would have given me the money if I'd asked, but I was sure that cash would arrive from somewhere. Which, thank God, it did.

I might be wrong about loans to people you know. Maybe there is no reason to worry. But I think most of us wish there were a way to avoid these situations. That's where the gift strategy comes in. Sometimes I ask why the borrower needs the money. He may talk about bills piling up. I may not be able to give him all he needs, but I'll say, "How much is your rent?"

He'll tell me the amount. I'll say, "Bring your payment book, and I'll write a check for the next two months. That should help."

In this way the money goes to the right place. Needy people may intend to take money to pay for essentials such as housing, utilities, and food. But they can be overwhelmed and distracted by financial pressure, and the loan they receive might not end up in the intended place.

If you pay an oppressive winter heating bill, you will know that your friend won't freeze to death.

I've asked for people's bills dozens of times, and never did I receive anything but an expression of gratitude and relief. Plus, there is real joy in paying rent or basic expenses for a good person in the midst of a struggle.

Proverbs 22:9 explains: "A generous man will himself be blessed, for he shares his food with the poor."

21

It's Your Funeral—Or Is It?

For some people, the only thing that scares them more than a trip to the hospital is the thought of a funeral.

Anyone's funeral.

That's because anyone's funeral makes people think of their own funerals, and who wants to spend a moment on that subject?

Have you ever been stuck having to plan someone's funeral? That has fallen to me twice, first for my mother, next for my father. When my mother died, it was from a sudden heart attack in 1984. At the time, my father was in shock. My brother and I helped my father pick out the casket. We sort of threw together a service, a few words from a minister spoken at the funeral home, then a quick graveside service.

It seemed as if we just went through motions. It didn't especially honor my mother. We had no idea what, if anything, she would have liked for a funeral. No family members spoke at the quick service. We just endured it, wanting it to be over. I knew that my mother was dead, and in the end what did it really matter to her what happened at the funeral?

What does any of this have to do with living our faith?

Consider this passage from the Old Testament, Ecclesiastes 7:2–3: "It is better to go to a house of mourning than a house of feasting, for death is the destiny of every man; the living should take this to heart."

When my father died in 1997 I was determined that the service would reflect his life and that it would say something about him, even if I had to say it myself.

Which is what ended up happening.

As I was planning my father's funeral, I remembered attending the funeral of Nev Chandler, the former Cleveland Browns announcer and TV broadcaster. Chandler was one of the finest men in the media business, where it's easy for egos to clash and grudges to form. Chandler was respectful and open to me when I was still attending Cleveland State and working in public relations for the long-gone Cleveland Cobras soccer team. There was no reason for him to be nice to me, other than Nev Chandler believed in being nice to everyone.

He died after a long duel with cancer at the age of forty-seven. His funeral was a combination of the spiritual hope of heaven and remembrances of family and friends. His brother served as a master of ceremonies. Nev's funeral was a celebration of Nev's life, a tribute to the way he faced death without blinking.

I had a sense that Nev had a hand in the service. For months he had known the end was near. Nev wanted everyone to have a good time when he was with them. His funeral was as much laughter as tears, and there was an abundance of both. It was a great gift to his family and friends.

Thinking of Nev Chandler's funeral reminds me of this verse from Isaiah 25:8: "He will swallow up death forever, the Sovereign Lord wipe away the tears from all faces."

Or, as Jesus said in John 11:25: "I am the resurrection and the life, he who believes in me will live, even though he dies. Whoever lives and believes in me will never die."

That was one of the messages of my father's funeral. His nearly five-year struggle with a stroke brought our entire family closer to God. It was the first time that I made a true, heartfelt commitment to being a Christian. My wife would say the same.

A week before he died, my father talked on the phone with a man named Fred Perkins, who, along with his wife, was instrumental in bringing a new, real faith to Roberta and to me. Fred had known my father casually.

Even though the stroke had limited my father's vocabulary to words such as "man," "yep," and "no," he still liked to talk on the phone. Fred spoke at length that day to my father about forgiveness, about faith, about heaven, and about leaving bitterness behind. My father cried as he listened to Fred, and as they prayed together.

At the service, I asked Fred to speak about that last conversation, the time when my father made his final confession, his final peace with God and life. I remember Fred walking to the casket, putting his hand on it, and saying, "Tom is not in here. That's just the body, the shell. He is in heaven now, looking down and smiling at the people who love him."

We also had a priest speak at the funeral—Father Dominic from Cleveland's Benedictine High School. He had known my father. Benedictine was an important part of our family because my father, my brother, and I all graduated from there.

Then I spoke about "the lessons my father taught me."

The lessons had to do with the value of hard work, with knowing there would be times when life would not be fair. The lessons had to do with the grace my father showed after the stroke, when he dealt with being confined to diapers and a wheelchair, when he could barely speak, yet he showed more love than at any other time in his life. I don't remember much of what else I said, but I know that God gave me the power to speak for my father. And I know the funeral was something he would have wanted.

My father was buried not in a suit, but in his favorite Indians' jacket. Also in his casket was a copy of my book *The Curse of Rocky Colavito,* and a cross. We threw in his Indians' cap, something else he loved.

It was like Nev Chandler's funeral—there were as many laughs as tears.

In Revelations 21:4 we learn that "[God] will wipe away every tear from their eyes. There will be no more death or mourning or crying or pain, for the old order of things has passed away."

My wife's father left specific plans for how finances and other business matters were to be handled after his death. He also spent time on his own funeral so that burden would not fall to his family. He loved bagpipe music, and he picked songs to be played. He selected two of his favorite ministers to deliver the eulogy and conduct the service. He asked that his favorite psalms be read. Then there was a part where anyone in the family could speak. My wife sang; her sister Vicky read a poem that she had written. For his family the funeral was simple because Dr. Robert Monroe believed that it really was *his* funeral, and that taking care of basic details was a gift he could give them. He determined that his body was to be cremated, and he arranged that in advance so his family would not have to make that decision.

My father-in-law was able to do this because he believed that through his faith in God and Jesus Christ, earth wasn't his final home, as much as he truly did love life and his family and friends.

I love this line from 1 Corinthians 15:54–55: "Death has been swallowed up in victory. Where, O death, is your victory? Where, O death, is your sting?"

Funerals are a time of grief. Tears should be welcome. Hugs should abound. They also should be a time of celebration.

In my church a funeral is called the "Home-Going Service," which means just that, it's time for the person we love to go home.

Since we're all going there, why not do those we love a favor and help plan the trip?

22

Shopping for a Church

At some time or another in life, people need to find a new church. Perhaps you are new to an area, or maybe you need a new place to worship. You may want to start your spiritual life fresh. If you haven't gone to a church for years you may not be sure how to look.

To find a new church, you have to make the search a priority. You should look for a church as diligently as you do a new car, a new outfit, a new job. It's too easy to fall into the trap of going to a church because it's close to home or because your family always attended that church. You may need a new church because the old church has changed, or maybe *you* have changed.

There aren't any guidebooks for finding a new church, but here are some simple suggestions. Be willing to set aside a few months to visit several churches. You must realize that a place of worship is not about what the church can do for you. Seek a church where you can be involved, a church that first points you to God.

1. *The Church Is Not God.* We need to remember that. A good church points us *to* God. A good church is a place where we can learn more about God and our faith. A good church is where we can feel God in our lives, and see God in the lives of others. A good church is all these things, but the church can't be God.

2. *You Will Have a Bad Church Experience.* Everyone has had a bad time in church, or will. But we can't let a *phony* in

church stop us from connecting with God. Arlington Church of God Pastor Ron Fowler once said, "Ever work with a phony? Did you get a paycheck? Did the fact that you worked with a phony stop you from cashing the check to get the real money?"

3. *Not All Churches Are for Everyone.* I got a letter from someone who was upset because a certain church did not believe in allowing women in leadership. A lot of churches do have women leaders. Some churches are looking for more male leaders. Look elsewhere. Some people like loud, spirit-filled churches. Others prefer more quiet atmospheres. Find a style of worship that fits your personality. If you go to a quiet church and complain it's too quiet that's your problem. If you want a small place and you attend a megachurch, don't complain that it's too big. You knew that when you drove up.

4. *Talk to Friends Who Seem Happy with Their Churches.* Find out why your friends like their churches. Go to church with some of them. Do research. Look up the church on the Internet. Read about its core beliefs along with the biography and resume of the ministers and church leaders.

5. *Make Sure There Is Some Stability in the Church.* Some churches are bogged down with politics and internal battles. If a church continually changes pastors, that's probably not a good sign.

6. *The Pastor Is Not God.* Some churches are built solely on the charisma of the pastor. It's critical to have a dynamic leader, but that should not be the only reason to attend a church. Even the best leaders have weaknesses and failings. Be guarded about a church where no one else ever speaks except one preacher. The church must be bigger than any pastor.

7. *Think Out of the Denomination Box*. Suppose you have been away from church for a long time. Suppose you grew up in a certain denomination and just grew tired of it. When you look for a church, don't just stick with one denomination. Look around at others. Styles of worship have changed over the years. Feedback from friends is a good place to start this investigation.

8. *Don't Worry about the Length of the Service*. I've sat through forty-five-minute sermons that left me wanting more, and I've nearly fallen asleep during ten-minute sermons. It's not how *long* the message is, but how *good* it is. One seminary student asked his preaching professor, "How many points should a good sermon have?" The professor replied, "One is a good place to start." When looking for a church, consider a place where sermons are taken seriously, where they are well prepared and where they are delivered with some passion.

9. *Have Mercy on the Pastors and Church*. Have you heard this saying: "That church was absolutely perfect—then I joined and messed it up?" Anyone can have a bad day, and that includes pastors and people in church leadership roles. We should not act like a critic and analyze every song, every prayer, every word of every sermon. Churches are about us connecting to God, not putting together a production to play on Broadway.

10. *Be a Giver, Not a Taker*. Ask not what your church can do for you, but what you can do for your church. Okay, finding a new church is not that extreme. The church does need to meet certain basic needs. But you need to get involved: take a class, join a ministry, support others. We need to develop a relationship with our churches. You can't have a relationship with anyone or anything in just one hour a week.

23

Forgiveness Letters

It was the hardest writing that I've ever done. The forgiveness letters.

After I became serious about my faith, I realized that I owed some people an apology. Actually, I had known about the apologies for years, but I had ignored it. I could always make the "yes, but . . . " argument.

We've all heard that one.

"Yes, I messed up, but she never should have . . . and I'm not about to apologize until she does first."

The longer I lived in the land of "yes, but . . ." the less it seemed that I had done anything requiring an apology. I could always rationalize an action, often better than the best defense attorney.

When I was younger and working at a different paper, the boss who hired me was demoted. Someone else was hired as boss. He came from out of town and made some mistakes, primarily because of his inexperience as a supervisor and his unfamiliarity with the sports market. I did absolutely nothing to help him. In his way, he did reach out to me. Instead, I complained about my job. I talked to others behind his back. I offered him no mercy, no patience, nothing but headaches.

For years, I had him in the box labeled "yes, but . . . "

Yes, I was a jerk, but so was he. Yes, I gossiped about him, but he did the same to me. Yes, I was immature and acted like a spoiled brat at times, but. . . . You get the idea.

As I studied the Bible, I realized I needed to do a lot of work on asking others for forgiveness, and also forgiving others.

I knew that in Mark 11:25, Jesus said: "When you stand praying, if you hold anything against anyone, forgive him so that your father in heaven may forgive you of your sins." And there is Psalm 119:133: "Direct my footsteps according to your word, let no sin rule over me."

Finally, there was my heart. I was many years and several jobs removed from that time of my life, but I knew that I had done that man wrong. I also knew that it wasn't a question of who was more at fault. People of faith are called to apologize for our mistakes and poor decisions. The rest is between God and the others.

I thought about calling that former boss, but I prayed about it and decided it was best to write a letter. The reason was that I could say exactly what I meant, and not do it emotionally. It was the safest way to remove myself from "yes, but . . . "

Before writing I prayed, asking God to keep me away from "yes, but. . . . " I also prayed there would be no lame apology such as "*If* I offended you, then I'm sorry."

Ever get one of those? *If* I offended you? The word "if" means that if you're so sensitive, I *guess* I'm sorry. *If* you took something the wrong way, then I'm sorry. *If* you're not mature enough to handle it. . . . Any apology with "if" is no apology.

So I simply wrote the man a note about how I was fixated on my own career, my own needs, and my own desires at that time. I confessed that I had a poor attitude about him before he arrived based on things that I had heard, combined with anger that the person who had hired me and supported me suddenly had been given what I considered a raw deal.

I wrote that I knew he had needed help because he had been brought into a difficult situation, and that I knew all I did was make the situation worse. I admitted that I'd never given him a fair chance. I did not mention anything that I believe he did wrong, nor did I offer any excuse for my own behavior. I asked his forgiveness, and added that no response was necessary.

I didn't receive a note back. I had no idea what he thought of my letter, if he thought anything about it at all. I just felt a sense of relief, what I call God's smile and a pat on the back. I had forgiven the man for anything he had done, and I asked his forgiveness in return.

That's all we can do. We can't force anyone to forgive us. People might not be ready to forgive; maybe they never will be ready. Maybe they fall into the same trap that I sometimes do, thinking that if I forgive someone I'm somehow letting him or her "get away with it," whatever "it" was.

I have to remind myself of the old line that says, "You start out holding a grudge, but the grudge ends up holding you."

Or, as part of Psalm 32 reads: "When I kept silent, my bones wasted away through my groaning all day. For day and night, your hand was heavy upon me. My strength was sapped."

When I mailed the forgiveness letter to my former boss, I felt real freedom. About a year later, I ran into the man. He simply said, "I really appreciated your letter."

By that time, I had written about six other letters. God kept bringing things to mind, people I'd hurt, ethical shortcuts that I had taken. In one case, a guy called me after getting my letter and said, "I barely remember what you're writing about, but I thank you anyway."

In another, I had quoted someone in a book many, many years ago. The man thought he was speaking on background. I thought I had made it clear I was interviewing him and taping it. When the book was published, he was outraged. He admitted that he said the things that I had attributed to him in the book, but he said I knew it made no sense for him to go on the record with his comments. He was worried that his identification in my book could cost him his job. (It didn't.)

I had long forgotten that incident until I began to write the first forgiveness letters. Then his face came to mind. I dug out the old interview tape. Sure enough, I did not say directly that I was taping and planned to quote him for the book. I simply said I was writing a book and asked for some help. There was room for misunderstanding, and the fault was mine.

So I wrote him a letter too.

I didn't see this source for a few years, but when we did cross paths he was friendly to me. He never mentioned the letter. Neither did I. After making an apology, we shouldn't expect a medal or even a kind word. Just as our apology must have no excuses, we should view an apology we make as a gift to the other person with no strings or expectations attached.

I wrote a story that hurt someone deeply. I had known the man for years. I can say that it was not my intent to harm him, but it did. And if I had thought about the situation for a while, I never would have written the story. In the end, it was not a big deal; it was a very short story. But it mentioned a painful part of his life that he didn't need to see in print again. He was in a career crisis. He had helped me over the years and had reason to believe he deserved better treatment. I'd heard he was upset and called to apologize. He was angry; I was defensive and started with "Yes, but . . . "

His wounds were still raw. I talked to him a few times after that, and he was cool to me. He thought I'd broken a trust. I wrote him a couple of notes of apology, and never heard much again.

Not every forgiveness letter brings a happy ending, but each can be a start.

Why a letter?

Because with letters you can pick a time when you're calm and not rushed to write it. You can make sure it says exactly what it should, with no parts reading "Yes, but . . . "

I also like letters better than e-mail, because my tendency is to write e-mails quickly and too often send them off before they are ready. I've had to apologize to readers for some of my stupid responses to their e-mails. I've found that too much emotion can bubble over into a volcano in cyberspace.

A letter can be written on the computer, but then printed out. Pray about it, and then let your letter sit for a day before reading it again. Read it on paper, just as the person who receives it will. Ask God to show you if there is anything that needs to be changed.

Realize that you can be confessing to God as you write a forgiveness letter, so make it worthy of a God who has forgiven us for so much. Then realize when you mail the letter that you have taken a major step toward freedom from guilt and from feeling that something wasn't quite right.

Then let the letter—and the person—go.

24

Time for a Card?

I love my wife for a lot of reasons, and one of them is because she loves to write and send cards. When I travel, I often find several cards in my suitcase, the envelopes numbered so that I know in which order they should be opened.

I usually call her each morning from the road and open a card. I read it to her, and I'm moved by the time she takes to pick them, the personal notes that she encloses.

She does this for others too.

My wife writes cards and notes to so many people: relatives, friends, inmates from our prison ministry. If she hears about someone who is going through a tough time, she sends that person a card, even if she barely knows the person.

Many people have told me how Roberta's cards show up at just the right time when they needed a lift, just when the walls of life seemed to be closing in. Her cards may have appeared just when people felt depressed but they didn't know why. I know inmates who use postcards written by my wife as a lifeline. They look at pictures of the mountains or the ocean and think about the world outside. They read the encouraging Bible verses over and over. They stare at cards, holding them in their hands, and feel a bit of God's touch.

I thought about these cards when I was visiting a place called Victory Church in Lakeland, Florida. The pastor talked about a funeral for a woman who had been in the church for decades. He said about a thousand people were at her funeral because she had been involved in so many church activities. She didn't have a lot of money, didn't come from a family with much political clout. But she had great radar for pain. She seemed to hear God's voice whispering a name at just the moment the person in pain needed a card.

The pastor asked the estimated thousand people at the funeral how many of them had received a card from the woman who died. "About two-thirds of them stood up," said Pastor Wayne Blackburn. "And that's why there were a thousand people at her funeral."

How hard is it? You buy a card and a stamp. You put in a little time and thought.

Yet I rarely do it.

Most of us know little things mean a lot, but most of us don't want to make the effort to do those little things.

My friend Bill Glass signs his name with this Bible verse (Philippians 1:3): "I thank God every time I remember you."

Because Glass is a former pro football player and member of the 1964 NFL Champion Cleveland Browns, his autograph is in demand. The verse points people to one of the most encouraging books in the Bible. Paul wrote a letter to the Philippians (in Greece) when he was in prison. He tells them, "He who has begun a good work in you will carry it on to completion until the day of Jesus Christ . . . I have you in my heart; for whether I am in chains or defending and confirming the gospel, all of you share in God's grace with me."

He also writes about being determined to rejoice even when he's in prison.

Most humor in our negative world is a put-down of someone else. Men especially struggle with encouraging others, even though all of us long to hear that we are doing a good job, that we are loved, that someone out there is thinking about us.

I want to introduce you to someone named John Mark. Historians believe he was the product of a mixed marriage. His mother was a Jew, his father a Roman soldier who died when Mark was very young. His mother's name was Mary, and she had a big house in middle of town. This story is about two thousand years old, but it still can speak to you today.

John Mark eventually became known simply as Mark, the author of one of the four gospels in the New Testament. That's about all most people know of Mark. They don't know that the first time he appears in the Bible, he's scared and running. He's running from his faith, running as he sees Jesus captured on Holy Thursday evening. He's running with such fear that he runs right out of his clothes, one of those loose robes worn back then.

We can't know the pain it took for Mark to find God's purpose for his life. Or how Mark's mother must have prayed and wondered what her child would become. Mary filled her big house with many of the new Christians in Jerusalem. Peter, James, John, and Paul were regular guests, according to historians. She knew she needed a man to help her with her son. She didn't go shopping for a husband. She recruited Barnabas. Barnabas is called a cousin in the Bible, but some scholars say he may have been an uncle to Mark, the brother of Mary.

Mary wisely turned to a close relative; someone she could trust. The Bible talks about Barnabas as an "encourager" by nature. He is one of the unsung heroes of the Book of Acts, the story of the new Christian church written by Luke.

Barnabas shows up in Acts, chapter 9, where a convert named Paul has become a Christian—the same Paul who later wrote the letter to the Philippians. Paul had been a member of the Jewish ruling class that was persecuting the new church before he had a dramatic conversion. The Christians didn't trust him. But Barnabas took time to get to know Paul, and believed in him. He stood up for Paul in front of the doubting Christians. Since Barnabas had such a tremendous reputation in the church, they extended some of his credibility to Paul.

We all need a Barnabas. We need someone to say, "This is my friend. You can trust this person." We need someone to reflect God's faith in us, to remind us how God believes in us. Barnabas became a flesh-and-blood "card of encouragement."

One of my favorite parts of the Bible, Psalm 68:5–6, says: "A father to the fatherless, a defender of widows, is God in his holy dwelling. God sets the lonely in families, He brings forth prisoners with singing."

Barnabas believed this, lived this, and sometimes even suffered for it. Barnabas accepted people as they were, and tried to help them to become even better through encouragement.

Barnabas and Paul collaborated on a mission trip, and they took Mark along. Barnabas was creating his own "Psalm 68 family." When Paul became a Christian, he left most of his relatives behind. Barnabas adopted him as a spiritual brother. Mark needed the influence of a man in his life, and Barnabas became his spiritual father. Barnabas put the two of them together for a great adventure.

By training, Paul was a thinker and a warrior. Mark was different. Mark grew up wealthy, slept on a real bed, had good food, and had experienced nothing that would prepare him for the demands of carrying the message to the rural mountains. When Paul and Barnabas decided to head to Turkey (taking a road known for its robbers, snakes, and rocks), Mark had enough. He quit and returned home to his mother.

Mary, no doubt, was glad to have her son back safely. But there had to be some shame. Mary loved those strong Christian men who were at her house. She wanted her son to grow up like them, to be another Barnabas or another Peter. But he turned and ran just as he did when Jesus was arrested.

The Bible doesn't say much more about this until two years after the first mission trip. Paul wants to go out again with Barnabas. Barnabas wants to take Mark. Paul refuses, saying Mark left them last time and that Mark can not be counted upon. You can read about this in Acts 15. Barnabas had to be angry. He had backed Paul, and Paul was refusing to help Mark. Paul probably thought Barnabas was putting their mission at risk in a wild attempt to find a job for Mark, who had done nothing to deserve another chance. In the meantime, new believers were watching as two titans of the early church argued and split! Paul took a friend named Silas and went in one direction; Barnabas took Mark and went a different way.

Do you have a feeling that Mark's mother was praying that somehow God would make something good out of this mess?

Here's what we know happened next: Mark became close to Peter. When it came time for Peter to write of his experiences with Jesus, historians say Peter turned to Mark for help. Even though Mark wasn't physically strong, he had been educated, and Mark accepted the challenge when Peter needed a coauthor. While Mark's Gospel is named after Mark, most historians agree that it is primarily Peter's story. Mark got it down on paper.

Mark started without a biological father, but he ended up with two spiritual fathers—Barnabas and Peter!

There are no letters or gospels written by Barnabas in the Bible, but without him there probably would be no Paul and his letters, and no gospel of Mark. The lesson we learn from Barnabas is about encouraging people who need it.

We can do that with a phone call, or with a card. It might take much more, like being a part of a "Psalm 68 family." But we *can* encourage others. Just get out those cards!

25

Do You Mix Messages?

A friend told me about his daughter who scored thirty-two points in a high school basketball game. It was a career high for her and nearly broke a school record.

"As we were driving home," he said, "I told her what a great game she played and that I was proud of her."

Sounds go so far.

"But then I told her that she took too many jump shots. She could have scored even more had she taken the ball inside," he said.

And he knew he had made a mistake. His daughter's spirits dropped. He tried to compliment her again. Her team did win. She played a super game. He just wanted her to think about driving to the basket a little more.

One of my spiritual mentors is Bill Glass, the former Browns defensive end who has spent more than thirty years in prison ministry. We coauthored a book called *Champions for Life: The Power of a Father's Blessing*. As we were talking about different topics, he told me one of the messages close to his heart is this: When you want to bless someone, then bless him (or her).

My friend is an example of mixing his message and missing a blessing. When he watched his daughter score those thirty-two points he should have told her how proud he was of her. Period.

"Too often, we want to pretend we're coaches," Glass said. "A coach always holds back part of the blessing. No one ever plays a perfect game. There's always something that can be done better. It's great for coaches, whose job it is to squeeze out a better performance each time. But it stinks for fathers."

And for mothers.

And for friends.

Growing up the son of a minor league baseball player and having an older brother who is a coach, I was used to having my life critiqued. But life is not one constant job evaluation. For me, it's hard *not* to be critical when I'm trying to say something nice. It's bad enough having the player-coach blood in my veins, but as a sports columnist, I'm paid to deliver opinions and that makes it easy to be negative.

We've all had the experience where a teacher or supervisor is looking over our work. The authority figure starts saying something positive, then comes the word "but . . . " That's when we really pay attention—and get defensive.

"But" is like hitting the delete key on the computer; it erases everything that came before. All the good stuff just disappears from our hearts. We may remember that some good stuff was said, but we won't feel it. We'll *feel* the negative. We'll feel that we didn't quite measure up. We'll feel that we have to work even harder.

The girl who scored the thirty-two points may know that her dad complimented her play, but she'll *feel* that he was disappointed because she shot too often from the outside. That's not the result her dad wanted. It's not what she needed to hear. But so many of us struggle with how to compliment, how to touch someone's heart with encouraging words.

The girl's father knows he could have waited a couple of days to offer his suggestion. We know we don't need to drop all of our opinions all the time.

Glass believes that women generally have a better understanding of this "blessing" concept than men do. Women seem more comfortable expressing unconditional love.

Of course I've been around women who can nitpick. For example, the chicken was excellent, the potatoes tasty, the beans terrific. But didn't the rolls seem a little hard? Don't you think a little juice would have been a nice touch?

What's the point? The cook knocked herself out to fix a meal. Just bless her. Thank her. Let her *feel* good about what she did.

Some people like to go through life playing "Gotcha!" They seem to be looking for the one thing that isn't quite right, the area that could use some improvement. And those people are just the ones to point out the inadequacy.

Have you heard someone tell your pastor, "I really liked your sermon, and the people at the church are so nice, but I wish you could do something about the music"?

Maybe the music does need work, but when the minister has just poured out his or her heart in the service, it is *not* the time to bring up the music.

Just bless people.

If we really care about people we should end every conversation with something positive. Glass believes parents should "bless their children" each night by telling them, "I love you. I will always love you. I think you are terrific. You are mine."

He says parents should do this even if it has just been an awful day. The day should end with a blessing. And we should do the same with family and friends. Speak a blessing into their lives. Tell them that we love them, that we appreciate how they have supported us, that they make our lives better.

How often do we say things like this to people who really matter to us? Probably not often enough.

Never assume that your loved ones know how you feel about them. Tell them how you feel even if it seems that they're not really listening. We all like to hear positive words spoken into our lives even if we shrug them off or act a little embarrassed by them.

Proverbs 15:30 reads: "A cheerful look brings joy to the heart, and good news gives health to the bones." Our words can touch people. They can make or break someone's day.

Does anyone really believe that "sticks and stones can break my bones, but words can never hurt me"? If we've ever been called "stupid," "lazy," "timid," or any other negative label, we know better. Those aren't blessings, they're curses.

So what about times when there are problems in a relationship? If we've been blessing people, if we have the courage to compliment and to express real love, then we can manage this kind of difficult discussion.

Don't bother with all the compliments because the "but" is coming and "but" is just like the delete key. Say something like, "I have to talk to you about this. You know when you forgot to pick up those things at the store, and then you didn't even apologize when I mentioned it—well, that hurt me."

If we have been unconditionally blessing our spouse, or friends, they are far more likely to accept criticism. They will know that we're not always being critical or looking for a reason to put them down.

In other situations when we need to be negative, we should try to attack the action, not the person. Don't say, "I can't believe how dumb you were to mess up that deal."

Say, "That deal didn't happen as it should have. I want you to tell me what went wrong. Then I'll give you my ideas."

One of the best ways to have a difficult conversation is to get the other person to speak first. Don't ambush him. Make it clear there are problems that must be addressed, then let him explain first.

This works for discussions in business, in marriage, with families or friends. With unconditional blessings we need to listen, really listen. We shouldn't just bite our tongues waiting for a chance to give our opinion.

Bill Glass has this rule, which I endorse: "Whenever possible, bless. If you're not sure if it's better to be critical or to bless, then bless. If you are going to discipline, then discipline. Whatever you do, avoid the mixed message."

26

Just Say, "Thank You"

Have you ever tried to give someone a gift? It could be a compliment. It could be money. It could even be a smile.

Some people just don't know what to do with it.

I'm one of those people.

Several years ago, a reader was trying to compliment me about a story I had written. I started to tell her how it could have been better, how there was a problem here, something that went wrong over there.

She seemed embarrassed. I just talked more about what was wrong with the story, a story she liked. A friend saw this and later said, "You needed two words."

I stared at him. "Just say, 'Thank you,'" he said.

I started to explain about the story again, but he held up his hand.

"Too much information," he said. "She was trying to be nice. She liked the story. Thank her and shut up. Is that so hard?"

It shouldn't be.

I've learned to do it, at least by e-mail. A reader sends me some kind words, and I simply reply, "thank you." I do it even if I know the story wasn't close to my best work. I do it because I remember what a veteran writer told me years ago. I do it because it drives me crazy when I try to compliment someone, and he or she just won't accept it.

One of the best ways that I've developed to answer a compliment is to say, "You really did make my day."

Or I say, "Today I needed some kind words."

But we all have moments when we really don't get it. Someone tries to compliment a woman about her dress and she says, "This old thing?"

Another woman told me that when someone compliments her clothing, "I'm afraid they'll think I'm rich and I paid too much for it, so I start telling them how much it cost and . . . "

I find myself falling into this trap, too. I bought a book for a child who is very close to my family. His mother said, "This is great! Where did you get it? He'll love it. This is really thoughtful."

She was sincerely gushing. I should have said, "Thanks, I'm glad to do it." Instead, I went on about finding it in a discount bin at a drugstore. It was priced at one dollar, but I had one of those special cards and got it for forty-nine cents.

She stared at me and said, "I don't care what it cost; he'll love it."

Just what was my problem? Was I feeling guilty because she was so happy with a forty-nine-cent gift? Was I trying to be humble? Was I bragging about getting a bargain? I really don't know.

Pastor Knute Larson of the Chapel said, "Some people grew up in situations where they received so little positive reinforcement, they don't believe it when someone compliments them."

That seems true. Or we were raised in such chaos that we assume a compliment is not a compliment; it's a way to manipulate us to do a favor for someone.

Sometimes, we're just clueless.

"I know that just saying 'thank you' is hard for me," said Rabbi Stephen Grundfast of Akron's Beth El Congregation. "I tend to be self-critical. We're all a little broken, and none of us is perfect. So we may think we really don't deserve it."

The rabbi paused for a moment. "Sometimes, I think about it too much," he said.

Most compliments are not that deep. Someone saw something he or she liked, and said so. We can return the compliment simply by accepting it with grace and without a long explanation.

Why can't I remember that?

One person recently complimented me about an Ohio State football story. I began a long, semicoherent response about how I had wanted to interview the coach, but missed him. And how I had wanted to write in the press box, but it was locked. And how I ended up writing it in a truck stop about forty miles from Columbus. And how I . . .

At that point the person seemed in need of smelling salts. Her eyes glazed, and she probably was praying for me to shut up so we both could leave. She must have thought, "I'll never compliment him again!"

Who can blame her?

Keep in mind, some people are just grouches.

You say, "You look very nice today."

They say, "What? I don't look nice on other days?"

Forget them. Their attitude is their problem, not yours. That kind of attitude is partly because we live in a sarcastic society, according to Larson.

"In basketball, you may throw up an air ball and someone says, 'Nice shot,'" Larson said. "They obviously don't mean it."

Larson added that there is an unwritten rule for the staff at the Chapel: "No sarcasm. Don't put people down that way. Don't make them wonder what you're really trying to say."

Sarcasm can be very destructive. It may be why some of us are a little paranoid. We receive a compliment and wonder, "Are they really putting us down? If I fall for this, will I look like a fool? Can this person really be sincere?"

Assuming the compliment is sincere, most of us can do a better job of receiving compliments more gracefully. And, we need to compliment each other more.

Philippians 4:8 reads: "Whatever is true, whatever is noble, whatever is right, whatever is pure, whatever is lovely, whatever is admirable . . . if anything is excellent or praiseworthy . . . think about such things."

And mention them to others.

Larson believes we should spend more time complimenting character traits, rather than what we're wearing or the cars we're driving. Tell people that you appreciate their patience, their wisdom, their kind hearts.

And when someone compliments you, just accept it.

Proverbs 15:23 reads: "A man finds joy in giving an apt reply—and how good is a timely word!"

One of the most timely words is "Thanks."

27

There's Not Enough Time . . .

Every time you say yes to something, you say no to something else.

Maybe that's obvious to you, or maybe you're just saying, "So what?" I came across this when I was reading *The 7 Habits of Highly Effective People*. Author Stephen Covey mentioned this idea in passing.

"Yes" to something means "no" to something else.

When I said yes to a request that I speak to a group, I said no to staying home that night with my wife.

Again, so what?

Knowing that when we say yes to something, we say no to something else can help us make better decisions. It can force us to really look at each chunk of time we commit, each evening away from home, and so on. Often, the request overpowers other parts of our lives. I know that I'm tired. I know that I need to stay at home and connect with my life. I know that I haven't been reading the Bible or doing anything else that would bring me closer to God. I know that I have been going too fast, and I need to slow down.

Then someone asks me to work more. It may not be a pressing assignment. I can turn it down and not create a real problem. But part of me wants to please my boss, and besides, I love my job. So I say yes.

The problem is I often say yes to things without really considering what I've just said no to, and how that will affect my family and me. It's not a bad idea to make a list.

For example, I will do the extra work. I won't be paid

extra; it's mostly a favor to the boss. I'm saying yes to him. I'm also saying yes to writing, which is a passion. All of that sounds good.

But I'm also saying no . . . to my wife, and we really do need to talk because I've been traveling a lot and working too many hours.

I'm also saying no to my body, which needs rest. No to my soul, which needs to be refreshed.

So look at the bottom line: Yes to job, boss, and writing. Not bad things.

No to wife, God, and myself. Even better things than my job.

If I did this type of list more often, I'd make better decisions because it would force me to really consider options. Sometimes, we all have to say no to our families. We have an emergency situation on the job, and we really are needed. Or we need to work overtime for the money because the cash flow is tight. It's okay to work, assuming we don't always put work first.

Proverbs 23:4 reads: "Do not wear yourself out to get rich, have wisdom and show restraint."

For some of us, work and money can be as addicting as crack cocaine. We can just want more and more, which means less and less of everything else.

Considering the no for every yes also is an excellent way to consider how we spend money. Every few years, I want to buy a new car. I drive a lot, at least 35,000 miles a year. I get a little nervous when my car rolls over 100,000 miles. Or at least I use that as an excuse to get a new car every three years or so.

I've never asked, "If I say yes to a new car, I'm saying no to what?"

I simply ask if I can afford it. I don't really consider what I can do with that money if I try to go another year with my old car, which is still in decent shape. And do I really need to take on another car payment, simply because I think I can handle it? Saying yes to the car also means saying yes to some debt, and perhaps no to things such as vacation or a donation. Maybe both.

Let's look at it this way: Is saying yes to a new dress saying no to something that really is more pressing? What if you buy clothes or other non-necessities on a credit card? As Proverbs 22:7 reads: "The borrower is servant to the lender."

And someone once told me, "It's easy to become a slave to credit cards. That's why they call it a MasterCard. It becomes our master."

My biggest battle is with time. How to spend it? Where to spend it? What is really worth my time? And why does it seem that I waste so much of it?

Have you ever wished you could cut yourself into pieces and be in three places at once? You are asked to attend a meeting for a good cause. A close friend says she needs your help. But your kids have a soccer game. Your mom needs a phone call, and you haven't talked to her for a week.

But the meeting is to help raise money for some special needs, and your friend is a real saint—always there to help you. Remember, if you say yes to something, you say no to something else. You go to the soccer game; that's a yes to your kids. It's not always a good idea to say yes to your children when it comes to giving them stuff, but it's rarely a mistake to say yes when it comes to spending time with them.

But you end up saying no to your friend, and that hurts. Maybe you try to call your mom from the soccer game, but you're on the cell phone, the reception is lousy, your attention is divided. You hang up knowing that your mom deserved more than that. You feel a little guilty.

You haven't even thought about the fact that what you really need is a night at home where you do nothing but take a bath, read a book, maybe watch a little mindless TV. You sigh and say, "That will have to wait until I'm retired."

A great prayer for this is in Psalm 31:14–15: "But I trust in you, O Lord; I say you are my God. My times are in your hands." In the end, that's true because when we die, we're out of time. But what about until the end?

"Some people controlled my time better than I did because I had not taken the initiative to command my time before they got to me," wrote Gordon MacDonald in his excellent book, *Ordering Your Private World*. I've read the book once, and gone back to it a few times. MacDonald also wrote, "I find myself doing small, unproductive and boring things just to get something accomplished."

Ever fall into that trap?

As a writer, I have. I was bogged down for several weeks on this book. I'd answer e-mails. I'd read other books. I'd pretend I was doing research, when I was really avoiding the mission in front of me—the book.

Ever been in an important conversation or working on a critical project when you're interrupted by the cell phone? We know we should let the caller leave a message, but we pick it up anyway. Suddenly, we are in a dumb discussion that could have waited hours, if not days. When we return to what we were doing, we're frustrated, distracted, and ineffective.

Why did we ever say yes to that phone call, especially when we said no to what really mattered? Was it simply because the phone made noise? Or was it because we wanted to get away from what we should have been doing even if it was demanding?

"God, my time is in your hands."

Ever pray that? I never had until seeing that verse one recent Thursday night. By Friday, my own stupid scheduling overwhelmed me. Most of the time, I know what's important. I just don't act like it. I spend too much time on the Internet, answering e-mails and checking out some website for information I don't need right now and could easily get the next day. Then I get mad at myself for wasting time.

"God, my time is in your hands."

I really do mean it. I just need God's help to act like it.

- 28 -

Sharing Your Faith

Do you ever want to talk to someone about God? Have you ever had someone try to talk to you about God with you feeling as if you'd like to whack the person over the head with the big Bible he's carrying around?

When I was considering writing about discussing faith with people, a friend simply said: "*Don't.*"

"Don't?" I asked.

"Just keep it to yourself," he said. "Too many people are trying to shove religion down our throats already."

I know people who enjoy walking up to strangers and asking, "If you died tonight, do you know if you'd go to heaven?"

While that's an interesting question, I doubt it has led to many serious discussions about faith. It's not quite as obnoxious, though, as the guy on the corner with the bullhorn spewing Bible verses and demanding that we repent on the spot or go straight to hell. Do these efforts help people connect with God?

Let's consider the question again: Should we even talk about faith?

The answer is yes. That's because it's a subject that's close to the hearts of many people, even if it doesn't seem to be on the tip of their tongues. If you bring it up the right way, at the right time, you may be surprised how people respond (and I don't mean with a frying pan to the side of the head).

Consider the August 29, 2005, issue of *Newsweek*, about half of which was devoted to "Spirituality in America." The magazine surveyed 1,004 people and discovered that 84 percent consider spirituality "important or somewhat important" in their daily lives.

Only 8 percent of those surveyed said they aren't "religious" or "spiritual."

Even if spirituality means different things to different people it's obvious that people are thinking about God. They are asking big questions. They are trying to pray. In fact, *Newsweek* discovered that 64 percent of those surveyed said they pray every day. Another 29 percent said they meditate. And 20 percent said they read the Bible, Quran, or some other sacred scriptures daily. As *Newsweek* related, America has come a long way from 1966, when *Time* magazine published a cover story asking "Is God Dead?"

Something is happening, and it can't be measured only by church and temple attendance. Most people know that there is a God. They may have a very clear vision of God, or they may have just a vague feeling about a Supreme Power, a Great Designer behind the mysteries of life and the universe.

I was talking about this with a casual friend who had long given up on church. I think he also has written off God, although I'm not sure. He's reluctant to talk about his personal beliefs, and I don't sense it's time to push. Yet, he reads all my faith stories. He likes to talk about the ones that have a clear application to everyday life. He has no interest in church or in prayer, but he'll talk about stories that I've written about prayer. It's fascinating, and we just keep talking. I'd love to help him come to a closer relationship with God, to give Christianity another chance. I'd like to point him to some good churches. But I can tell that he wants to talk, so we talk. I like him as a person, a smart, thoughtful guy no matter if he's talking sports, politics, or education.

I mentioned that faith changed my life, made me more considerate of others, and strengthened my marriage. If faith has no value, no impact on your behavior, then what good is it?

Or as James wrote in the New Testament: "Faith without works is dead." A modern translation of James's line might be this: "Does your walk match your talk?"

That is a problem many people have, especially with churches. The walk doesn't come close to matching the talk. When I hear that, the first thing I do is admit I don't have all the answers. I say that anyone who claims to know everything about God makes me nervous, and I tend to avoid those people.

Often, people will say, "I have some real issues with churches."

I say, "I do, too."

This usually surprises them. They expect me to defend every church, every preacher, and every con man with a religious TV show. I don't spend much time criticizing these types, but when someone is obviously out of bounds, I'll say it.

That surprises people, too. Then I'll say that it wasn't much different in the time of Jesus. His harshest words were aimed at some of the religious establishment.

"I try not to let phonies in church get between me and a real God," I say.

People who may be turned off by religious leaders may be interested in getting closer to God. They may want to know if God cares about them and if that can change and improve their lives. Those topics are worth talking about. They also can lead to discussion about how to have a personal relationship with God, how to talk to God in prayer, how a prayer can be just those conversations we have in our heads during the day.

Instead of talking to ourselves—and we all do—talk to God. See what happens.

Still, no one should be forced to discuss faith. If you bring up the subject and your listener isn't interested he or she will shut you down. Honor that. Just let it go. Don't make people uneasy. Don't force your beliefs on them. Don't think you can have a decent conversation about God simply with the power of your will or your theological knowledge.

Finally, don't start telling others how to live their lives because they will immediately begin to look at your life and find inconsistencies. And yes, we all have them. There are moments when I'm astounded by my own hypocrisy. I can gossip. I can swear. I can rip into someone with absolutely no mercy. Sometimes it seems that I'm not even making a token effort to follow God's commandments.

In fact, when I've admitted that to people, they've often appreciated it.

I say, "I don't like it when I act that way. I try to immediately ask the person and God for forgiveness. I sometimes get sick of me and my mistakes. But I am working on all of it, and I'm praying about it. I want God to make me a better person, and I know that I have to help.

We have to be aware that we're just not going to reach some people. We have too much history with them, too much baggage. A young woman wrote me about how she'd love to tell her family about her faith. She has a physical disability, and her Christianity has helped her overcome her anger about it. Her church has given her a real community with friends who care about her. Prayer helps her deal with frustration. But her family just doesn't want to hear it.

I told her, "Sometimes, the hardest people to reach are our relatives. They know us too well. They often are in competition with us, or they resent us about something. Pray for someone else to talk to them at the right time, then just back off and be friendly."

The idea is not to convert people. It's not to force them to do anything. It is to find out if they are on a spiritual journey, and if so, ask whether they would mind if we talk about it. *Newsweek* found that 39 percent of people say they "practice religion" to "forge a personal relationship with God." Another 10 percent said it's to "connect with something larger than yourself."

Add that up and it's roughly 50 percent of the people surveyed. Many of these people would be delighted to have a serious, nonthreatening conversation about God.

What is a good way to do that?

According to *Newsweek*, we live in a country where 64 percent of people surveyed said they pray daily, and 80 percent said they believe we are created by God. So why not talk a little about prayer? Why not ask someone who is hurting if she would mind if you prayed with her? I tell people that prayer is strange and that I don't know how it works. I have no idea why some prayers are answered and others are not. Nor am I sure how God responds to our prayers; I just pray anyway.

Maybe that's not a strong intellectual argument, but it's honest. People usually appreciate that. Most of the time they'll say, "I guess it's okay if you want to pray for me."

I'll do it on the spot (or on the phone). I'll just talk to God as if he were in the room with me. I'll keep the prayer short, personal, and direct. It may be something like "Father, you know that Sara is having problems with her son. You know how her heart aches for him. You know she isn't even sure what to do anymore. She's just worried he'll get into real trouble. I don't really know how to pray for him, but you know what he needs. So I just put him in your hands. And I pray for Sara. Give her comfort. Give her hope. Help her to sleep at night. Help her to deal with the problems of the day. Give her wisdom and patience and send her people to encourage her."

I'll often end that type of prayer with "In the name of Jesus, amen."

A few years ago, I wrote a two-part series on unanswered prayers suggesting that spiritual leaders discuss the subject from the pulpit. Readers agreed, and had their own stories about how they handled it when it seemed God wasn't there for them. Many of them keep believing and praying anyway, often because they remember when God did come through for them.

Sometimes people might consider going to church, but they don't know where to go. They may have had bad church experiences, and they really don't want to try it on their own. I've seen surveys that showed people would consider going to church with a person they respect, but that person has never asked.

If you do ask people to go to church and they seem upset or bothered, quickly back off. Just keep talking about things that matter to them. If these are your friends or people you care about, you should treat them as friends and show them you care. Don't act like you are out to make a sale. If you don't care and don't want to take time to get to know people, then don't bother with the discussion. Why open the spiritual door, yet refuse to help people walk through it?

Too many people talk about faith, invite people to church, and then sort of back off. They seem to think: "Now it's between her and the church," or him and the pastor. But if you are the one who introduced someone to church and to God, stay with her, keep listening to him, keep talking and keep praying.

Finally, remember that all of us are searching for something. We can be there to help each other, especially when it comes to connecting with God.

A Conversation with Terry Pluto

1. This is your second book dealing with faith. What compels you—a popular, successful sports columnist—to write about values?

People care about values. Most people want to make a connection with God. Most people would say they're on a spiritual journey. People in newspapers are afraid to get anywhere near that subject for fear of offending someone. My approach is to say that I don't know everything about God, but I'm on journey too. I want to know how to live. I want to live a life that is pleasing to God even if I'm not always sure what God wants from me. Bring that subject up and you can usually get people talking about faith without wanting to kill each other.

2. What is your definition of Everyday Faith?

Where you spend your time and your money tells a lot about Everyday Faith. Faith is not just something that floats out there above our heads. It's not a vague theology question, or one religious group throwing theological spitballs at another. It's about how you live your life, how you handle suffering, how patient you are with others. It's not easy to live out our faith every day, but most people really do want to do it.

3. Your parents, brother, wife, and other family members appear in many of these chapters. How would you describe the role of family in your own faith life?

My parents had what would be considered a mixed marriage. They came from two different denominations, so I never had one set doctrine drilled into my head. My mother died in 1984 of a heart attack, and my father died in 1998 after he suffered a stroke nearly five years before. It was during that time taking care of my father, which took an incredible amount of time and money, that I began to look to God because I often felt like I had nowhere else to go.

4. How do you think families can build their Everyday Faith?

Children watch how their parents live every day. They have tremendous capacity to sense hypocrisy and inconsistency, but they also have a real longing to connect with God. Parents often are the first glimpse at God that children will ever have. So by praying together, talking about values, and encouraging each other through the little things and the big crises, that's how you show faith in families.

A good church should operate as a family, too. Part of it may seem a little dysfunctional, just as no family is perfect. But ideally a church and a family should both help us get through the battles that we face every day.

5. What is the most difficult faith issue you personally face?

To be humble enough to admit I don't know everything about faith, sports, money, or anything else I find myself talking about. When you write for a newspaper and you're a columnist paid to give your opinion, you find that it comes naturally to assume you're an expert. And just because you write about an issue doesn't mean you're the final authority on it.

The hardest thing for me to do is listen. It can be reading the Bible and then trying to be quiet and hear something from God, or trying to be quiet and listen nonjudgmentally to what my wife is trying to tell me about something that happened in her day or some problem she's facing.

6. So many of your Everyday Faith messages are not just spiritual or religious ideas, but commonsense advice. Why is that?

I have an advantage not being in full-time ministry. Most readers think I'm living in the same world as them. Clergy also live in the same world we do, but the perception is that clergy are somehow immune to the pressures that most of us face. But a guy who's a sportswriter, whose father had a stroke, and who wants to have a good marriage, is something that a lot of people can relate to. Most people want to have better relationships, most people have personal crises, most people want to know how to live a life of faith that makes sense and is real. Real faith is God-guided common sense.

7. Changing to or leading a more faith-filled life can seem like a daunting challenge. If you could suggest just one thing people could do to improve their faith lives, what would that be?

Most people are afraid of changing anything significant in their lives. Having worked for almost eight years in prisons, where 80 percent of the people are addicted, I can tell you that there are no real behavior changes until the pain of living a certain way becomes greater than the fear of change. This is not an original idea. I've heard it expressed in different ways, but it's true for all of us. We don't want to change our budgets because we're used to spending money in a certain way, even when it's clear we're spending far too much. We don't want to change our wardrobes because we've always dressed a certain way, even when it's obvious that our clothes no longer fit. So it's scary to think about changing something that's as close to us as the values that determine how we live. That's why it's called "faith." There's a verse in the Bible that says, "We walk by faith and not by sight." I don't care if you're an addict, a shopaholic, or someone who feels something is just not right in your life. You'll only change when you get tired of the pain, but it's out of pain that the greatest change comes.

Sometimes people are afraid that if their faith grows God will want them to go to India or somewhere and work with the poor or sell all their possessions and live in a cardboard box. Most of the time God wants us to live in our same houses and work in the same places, but just change how we act and how we think. In other words, most of our exterior remains the same; the change is inside us. In the Old Testament there are several verses that say, in essence, "God will give you a new heart." And that gives you the faith to try something a little different.

8. How did you get started in prison ministry?

It began when I did a story for the *Beacon Journal* on Bill Glass, the former Browns defensive end who has spent more than thirty years in prison ministry since retiring from football. I met Glass at Chicago's Cook County Jail to spend a day with him, and then I wrote the story and figured not much would come of it (just another of the three hundred stories I write each year). Then I got a call from a chaplain at the Summit County Jail in Ohio asking me if I wanted to visit the jail during the Christmas holiday and help them pass out shoeboxes to the inmates. In the shoeboxes were cookies, a Bible, some socks, a stamped envelope, and some stationery. The idea was that the inmates could use the paper to write a letter to someone in their family. The socks were valuable in jail because at Summit County all the inmates wear shower slippers. Some of the inmates didn't have socks, and their feet got cold during the winter. Then, the inmates were always looking for something to read, so they gave them the Bible. The cookies were a treat that was approved by the authorities.

Former Akron University football coach Lee Owens went with me that first time and brought a couple of his players to help pass out the shoeboxes and shake hands with the inmates. Most of the inmates knew who I was because there were lots of *Beacon Journal*s around the jail and because many of the inmates were sports fans. I had an instant audience. I was a new Christian at the time—probably only six months into becoming serious about Christ—and the chaplain asked me if I'd come and speak at the next Sunday night jail service. I realized then how overmatched I was. But I went because I felt drawn to those guys, many of whom looked just like me. Prison ministry is terrific because most of the inmates are just so glad to see anybody who isn't a prosecutor, a deputy, or some other legal type. Those who go to the chapel service volunteer to go, so it's not forced on them. They don't think they're perfect, and they don't expect you to be perfect. It really is a classic case of "We're all sinners and searchers looking to get closer to God and just trying to get through today."

People think jail ministry can be dangerous, but just the opposite is true. It's one of the safest places to be if you're a volunteer. In jails, volunteer ministers and teachers are in a special class, which is very respected even by those who aren't interested in faith or the classes. You're not viewed as part of the system; you're seen as someone who is there to help. I met this one inmate who used to be a member of the Aryan Brotherhood, or white skinheads, until he became a Christian. He told me: "If anybody touches you guys [the volunteers], we'll kill him." He meant that they wanted us to feel safe and comfortable coming to see them.

I've been in jails at least five hundred times in my life and never had anything resembling a physical confrontation. The inmates may fight each other; some will even fight the deputies. But that inmate was right. They won't touch us. If anything, they're overprotective. That shows that most of these guys can live a pretty good life if they're not drinking or drugging or trying to get money to drink and use drugs. We just hope that our classes point them in that direction.

9. Do you think faith or religion has a place in sports?

I don't think God cares who wins the World Series or Super Bowl, but I do think God expects us to do our best with the ability he's given us. It doesn't matter if we're playing quarterback, writing about the game, or cutting the grass on the field. It never bothers me when a player thanks God that he has the ability to play. I'm not impressed when players say that God somehow favored their team to win. Does that mean God hates the other team? In many ways, I bet God has a soft spot in his heart for losers because those are the people that Jesus seemed to spend the most time with.

10. If you could recommend one place to start studying the Bible, where (or what part) would that be?

If you're suffering or going through a hard time in your life, start with the Psalms. They're nothing more than 150 prayers written by different people. You will be surprised about the raw emotion found in the Psalms. They are not the "church-ey" prayers that most people think. These show people going through loneliness, physical suffering, feelings of betrayal, or just the sheer joy of God doing something special in their lives. What the Psalms really do say is that all these people felt close enough to God to be truly "honest to God" in what they were thinking and feeling.

If you want to learn more about Christianity, read the gospels of Luke and John and ask yourself "Who is Jesus?" as you read them. Look at the people Jesus picked as his disciples and notice that they were very flawed and that he had lots of patience with them.

Finally, the most practical advice in the Bible is found in the Book of Proverbs. It tells you everything from how to raise your kids to how to handle money.

If you've never read the Bible before, or it's been a long time since you opened it, there are some excellent translations in modern English that really make it easy to understand. I like the version called the New International Version, but there are several others that are very good. Some people like the traditional King James and there's nothing wrong with that; in fact, it's my wife's favorite. Just find a translation of the Bible that really speaks to you, and be willing to spend a few extra bucks for a study Bible that will supply lots of background information that helps put everything into context. .

11. Who is your favorite person or character in the Bible, and why?

Moses, because he was a guy who was eighty years old when God suddenly put a call in his life to lead the Jews out of captivity in Egypt. He felt totally overwhelmed and underprepared for the task. He knew God well enough to argue with God, to bargain with God, and to beg God to send somebody else. But Moses was like a lot of us. In the end, he went and did what God asked because he had to, not because it was something he wanted to do. Moses walked in faith because he felt he had no other choice. He often had to deal with people who complained. He was sometimes accused unfairly and was the subject of awful rumors.

The story of Moses also gives us hope that God is liable to call on us at any point in our lives to do something extraordinary. It may not be leading people out of slavery, but it could be a grandparent helping a grandchild through a period when that child feels alienated from his parents or lost in school or just looking for somebody to hug him and listen. Moses is my hero because he figured out God's will for his life and did it even when it wasn't easy. I wish I could do that sometimes.

12. What is your favorite psalm? What is your favorite verse?

Psalm 142 was written by David when King Saul was trying to kill him. David was hiding in a cave, and he was worn out and feeling hopeless and betrayed. He was telling God all this, or as the psalm says, "I pour out all my complaints before him, before him I tell all my trouble." This tells me that God does care about how we're feeling. As David talked about his problems he began to remember the times God had been faithful to him, and David has this wonderful line that reads,

"Set me free from my prison that I may praise your name." I think all of us go through periods where we feel a "prison" that could be family pressures, money problems, career crises, or just feelings of loneliness. God is willing to meet us where we are, if we just call out to him.

My favorite Bible verse is 2 Corinthians 5:17: "If anyone is in Christ, he is a new creation. The old is gone, the new has come." I love that because it says God is not done with us yet; that we don't have to be the same person today that we were last week or ten years ago. It speaks of God's forgiveness. Some people may never forgive us, no matter how often we ask. But we do have a God who is willing to look at us as new people through the forgiveness that comes through faith in Christ. Often my biggest battle is not just believing that God forgives me, but being willing to forgive myself for some of my mistakes. So the verse reminds me that I am a new creation in Christ. The old is gone; the new has come. I bet I tell myself that three times a day.

Acknowledgments

My biggest thanks goes to Jan Leach, who had faith enough in me to start the "Everyday Faith" column in the *Beacon Journal*. Jan also edited this book, and *Everyday Faith*.

David Gray has been a terrific publisher, another with faith in me to write about God, faith, and other topics that make some publishers very nervous.

If there ever is a hall of fame for public relations people in publishing, Jane Lassar should be a first-ballot selection. She has been a tremendous blessing to me.

Brian Willse, who illustrated the cover for this book and for my previous book *Everyday Faith*, has a great eye.

My bosses at the *Beacon Journal* have also had great faith in me: publisher Jim Crutchfield, editor Debra Adams Simmons, and sports editor Larry Pantages. My religion editor is Mitch McKenney, a real encouragement to me. Sue Reynolds, Maribeth Lieberth, and Mary Lou Woodcock have been a real help to me at the *Beacon Journal*.

I have been represented by Faith Hamlin for more than twenty years, long before I ever imagined writing a faith book. She's always had faith in me.

I know a lot of pastors who have blessed me, but those who have made the most impact are Ronald Fowler, Diana Swoope, Joey Johnson, Knute Larson, and Bill Glass. You are my spiritual mentors and have been a real inspiration.

ABOUT THE AUTHOR

Terry Pluto is a faith and sports columnist for the *Akron Beacon Journal*. He also is the author of 22 books. He has twice been nominated for the Pulitzer Prize for commentary, has twice been named the nation's top sports columnist, and has been named Ohio Sportswriter of the Year eight times. He has also won an Amy award for his faith writing.

He and his wife, Roberta, help lead weekly prison ministry services at Summit County jail; they also volunteer at the Haven of Rest City Mission in Akron.